includes materials for all ages. It is both secular and sacred and contains directions for producing and arranging specific pieces of work. Information on music, dance, projections, costumes and lighting is also provided. I had a desire to make available materials for group reading and to help groups produce by giving directions and defining my philosophy gained from twenty years of experience with a touring group."

Theatre of the Word is an extensive volume, backed by many years of experience and research. It is divided up into distinct categories, some of which include organizing and choreographing the verse choir, selections for club functions, programs with a theme, and feature numbers for their visual and humorous effects. There are also a number of religious works taken from various documented sources.

Dr. England believes that choral reading improves good speech, interpretation, development of the personality, and a creative attitude towards life. She says this is a good tool for freeing the individual's capacity for self-awareness and creativity. Those interested in group reading will be invaluably rewarded by this book, a source which can be turned to again and again for insightful guidance. Even if you are in no way connected with this art form, maybe it's time to experience something new and uplifting.

THEATRE OF THE WORD:

THE LIVELY ART OF GROUP READING

THEATRE OF THE WORD:

THE LIVELY ART OF GROUP READING

THEORA C. ENGLAND

A Hearthstone Book

Carlton Press, Inc.   New York, N.Y.

© 1979 by Theora C. England
ALL RIGHTS RESERVED
Manufactured in the United States of America
ISBN 0-8062-0893-7

To my husband Harry L. England
an ardent fan of the Choral Readers
and to The Northwestern College Choral Readers
who served as inspiration for the book.

Now I make a leaf of voices
    For I have found nothing mightier than they are
And I have found no word spoken but is beautiful in
        its place.
        —Walt Whitman

A word
is Dead
when it
is said
some say.
I say
it first
begins
to live
that day.
    —Emily Dickinson

CONTENTS

List of Illustrations

Startling. . .vibrating. . .precarious. . .penetrating. . . unfolding. . . intoxicating. . .adjectives defining the art of making literature alive.

Perception. . .rhythm. . .balance. . .awareness. . .passion . . .power. . .nouns defining the essence of fine art.

Music. . .drama. . .dance. . .costume. . .writing. . .relation-ships. . .voice. . . feelings. . .instruments. . .painting. . .each a component of the fine arts—each an essential element of Choral Reading. With the possible exception of the Play— Choral Verse Speaking is the only fine art needing all the fine arts to succeed.

Choral Reading is not a group of people deciding to read something together. Churches do that with Responsive Readings and do it terribly. Great poetry and prose is not simply meant to be read. . .but be felt, touched and known inwardly and thus, spiritually. Great literature is created to expose life, stimulate life, change life, and help us at the bottom line to appreciate life.

Fine arts not capturing life are purposeless. You do not sing great songs simply to see how good you can sing. . .but to appreciate, and cause others to appreciate music's beauty. Fine Art seeks life's ideals and exposes us to the Creator's goodness.

Choral Reading, to my mind, is the zenith of Fine Art. It is not an individual standing alone in the spotlight receiving the adoring praises of the adulating mobs. It is coping with human relationships. . .striving to attain the inter-personal unity necessary to make literature live. Each group member must place his or her soul in common with the others so the group can unfold the literature's truth with power, inter-pretation and conviction. This cannot be done without the attendant skills of the other fine arts of costume, movement, voice, music, painting and expression.

No individual is graced with all the talents of the fine arts. The gifted actor must work with the shy intellect to discover the meaning of the work to be performed. The loner and the individualist is needed along with the popular and charis-matic. Each represents a stream of life and each contributes to the understanding of Choral Reading because each has experienced different slants on the literature used.

There is no qualification, no standard necessary to be a member of a Choral Reading Group except the desire to make literature live. This is how it was in Dr. England's groups. Choral Reading's demand for many talents and individuals brought in diverse people. The maladjusted and the not so good looking were just as important to the groups as the popular and beautiful. Somehow it all worked. Stutterers learned to speak normally with the group. Shy people became bold before hundreds. We learned to appreciate good literature and use our minds and bodies to reveal its life.

—Rev. Paul Nulton, a member of the Northwestern College Choral Readers, 1965-1969

Northwestern College Choral Readers—a lively art.

WHAT IS A VERSE CHOIR?

Solo —these differences may come to light when we ask,
"What is a verse choir?"

Chorus A verse choir is nothing, I guess,/
But a whole lot of people who want to more or less
TALK together / like this/
We have *light voices, medium, dark voices,*
We talk all together or sometimes just a few,/

Chorus And we'll say something now if we thought
that you/
Would like to hear some things to reMEMMMMber./

Solo Do we only hear three separate voice groups?
I thought we had four.

Chorus We do./ They are: *LIGHT, MEDIUM WOMEN,*
MEDIUM MEN, and DARK!

Solo Thank you. Now just to be more explicit could
you give us a sample of how each voice group can
be used to more effectively express a certain
thought or feeling—for instance the four moods in
Edgar Allan Poe's poem "The Bells"?

l Hear the sledges with the bells, SILVER bells!

mw Hear the mellow wedding bells, GOLDEN bells!
What a world of happiness their harmony foretells.

mm Hear the loud alarum bells, BRAZEN bells!
what a tale of terror now their turbulency tells!

d Hear the tolling of the bells, IRON bells!
What a world of solemn thought their melody compels!

Solo Thank you. These are the four divisions of our
choir, based on the inherent quality of the natural
speaking voice of each individual member. This
difference in voice quality is one of the seven
variables we use in trying to lift out the inner
meanings of a piece of literature for you.

San Diego Verse Choir
San Diego State College
Prof. E.K. Povenmire, director
reprinted by permission of Dr. Povenmire

ACKNOWLEDGMENTS

I wish to thank authors, publishers, and agents whose interest, co-operation, and permission to reprint materials have made possible this publication of *Theatre of the Word: The Lively Art of Group Reading.*

I thank former students and friends who have helped me with my research and have contributed their own original selections. Special thanks to the staff of Ramaker Library, Northwestern College.

INTRODUCTION

"...for it was not only a voice
of gold, but it was the voice of a
man whose heart was *golden*...
reading from a book of *golden
words*"
Cry, the Beloved Country, Alan
Paton.

The title of this book may raise a question in your mind. "When we went to school and encountered exercises in choric speech it was anything but a lively art!" More than likely we could have been labeled choral mumblers. My intent is to demonstrate, on the contrary, that group reading is a lively art and not a dull perfunctory recitation. It is a group of people experiencing together the joy of reading and interpreting the wealth of literature in harmony of voice, body, mind. It includes also the use of multi-media, art, music, dance, simple lighting, costuming, interesting vocal arrangements, and grouping of participants.

The principal tools for freeing the individual's capacity for self-awareness are creative activities. One of these activities is group reading. The participants have the opportunity of expressing themselves freely, openly, spontaneously, vibrantly in their own individual style, eventually giving way to cooperation achieved through group decision making. The most effective leadership comes from within the group and not necessarily from a group leader. Criticism by the group aroused through its own generated pride and enthusiasm is the goal rather than the dictatorship of a director or leader who is bent on his own techniques of style and form. The director should stress variety in interpretation of the material selected, crisp diction, rhythm, balance, thought, and relaxation of the body.

Incidentally, group reading does help to develop and bring out the personality of the shy and self-conscious individual and helps the overconfident person to become a part of the group, experiencing the creation of beauty.

When young folks are polled for their attitudes toward

choral reading, their typical responses are: "I find myself speaking with ease in all situations"; "I couldn't stand poetry but now it is my thing"; "I can commit to memory much faster"; "It inspires me and I am led to action in ways that I can not always explain"; "I find words fascinating, and it is fun playing with them"; and "You're not up there all by your lonesome." If a student has the opportunity for taking only one speech course, it should be choral reading, for it includes good speech, interpretation, development of the personality, and a creative attitude toward life and living.

I hope that among my readers there will be those who will feel free to explore and discover other ways of approaching the creative field of group reading. For as in all of the arts, it is an aesthetic adventure, an ever changing encounter with beauty.

THEATRE OF THE WORD:

THE LIVELY ART OF GROUP READING

ORGANIZING THE VERSE CHOIR

Poetry is the wisdom of the ages
It can be found in books on certain pages
To remove from it a vagueness or a cloud
It must be spoken often and aloud.

Group reading may be introduced to persons of any age. For children it is a means of enhancing their enjoyment of poetry. The teenage boy or girl had reached an awareness, a sensitivity to group reaction. He is ready and eager to receive the approval of an audience.

Verse choirs may be used successfully with college students. E.K. Povenmire of San Diego State College, states in his sabbatical study report:

Choric speech is a vital part of higher education in the United States at the present time. It is used as a part of other courses and activities, and as teacher education, theatre, voice and diction, music, and dance.

Dr. Ailene Cole, director of theatre at Augsburg College, Minneapolis, organized a verse choir at Cannon Falls High School, Cannon Falls, Minnesota. These young people participated in a Christmas program for eleven years in close cooperation with the mixed chorus and its director. The programs were presented on the stage of the gymnasium with the basketball bleachers placed thereon for seating. The chorus was seated on one side, and directed by the chorus leader it provided background music. The verse choir was placed on the opposite side and was dressed in white. On a platform above the choruses, pantomimed scenes were presented behind a scrim. Usually a church window, organ pipes or some other symbolic item was painted or projected on a background piece.

Dr. Cole wrote her own scripts and one of them, "Fall on Your Knees" is included in this book.

The Advent Readers were brought together to prepare a program for a Lenten service at the Advent Lutheran Church, Murfreesboro, Tennessee. Businessmen, housewives, teachers, college students and high school students became close and united, loyal to each other and to the purpose and ideals of the group. They found inspiration and enjoyment and a new dimension to their spiritual life in reading together and they continued their rehearsals and presentations after the Easter week service. Rev. Quail, the pastor, is also a member of the group. He uses the readers in his regular Sunday morning services to highlight some special message.

The Fiery Furnace with dancers.

28

The Chancel Readers, Spartanburg, South Carolina.

The Chancel Readers were organized in Spartanburg, South Carolina in the spring of 1977. The sponsor was The Christian Drama Group of this city and members came from various churches and denominations, and included persons from thirteen years of age to fifty. The Readers presented programs in North and South Carolina during the Lenten

Season with power and vitality, and audiences responded enthusiastically. Guitars, violins, drums, a flute, a gifted organist, and graceful dancers added variety and interest to the productions.

Mary Gwen Owen, drama instructor at Macalester College, St. Paul, and director of the magnetic Drama Choros is spending her retirement years in a productive way. She is employed at the State Training School in Red Wing, Minnesota under *New Focus: Arts and Correction*, a fine arts program under private and state grants.

Using her unique Drama Choros technique she directed six shows last year, including one for the legislature in the Rotunda of the State Capitol. Miss Owen says:

> It was an exhilarating experience, although a sad one, knowing that all these eager, normal looking lovely human beings had been battered—and under the facade one saw in class were disturbed, often suicide-prone children... They are losers and non-achievers. It is thrilling for them and for me to see them (girls in long scarlet skirts—boys in long scarlet vests, clean white blouses or turtle necks—shining and eager) whip to the stage and raise their books over bows to the audience ...They are desperately in need of love and understanding—of touching.

Miss Owen continues her thrilling story and concludes by saying..."there is no technique like group reading for creating excitement in a class."

Now we are approaching some of the methods for organization of a formal verse choir as we recognize the social, psychological and physiological values. This will become an avenue of expression far superior to mass riots and protest marchers.

Verse speaking may be introduced into adult groups, clubs and civic organizations. It is used extensively by church groups, in the chancel for worship, and in inner-city projects.

For all of these groups there are certain basic principles to insure a delightful and exciting performance with the least amount of humdrum phrasing, marking of pauses and

30

emphasis, and monotonous rehearsals. The rehearsals are necessary but should be spent on interpreting and developing ideas and techniques.

The first of these principles is Relaxation. Relaxation is at the base of endurance. In this high-tension age, more than ever, it is important that daily periods of relaxation be observed if the nervous system is to endure the strain. There must be relaxation of the whole person, body, mind and spirit, if the voice is to have a good chance.

What is the meaning of relaxation? Relaxation is the degree of tension present in the entire body. It is important in projecting to an audience. The muscle tone present reinforces or detracts from the speaking voice. Good posture is due to controlled relaxation. Relaxation is an easing of tension, not total disintegration, boredom, weariness, or depression.

Harmful tension is described as more tension than is needed to execute a movement or to maintain a position. Instruct your readers to use only the muscles needed to execute the task at hand. They should use the muscles needed to read, to stand, sit, bow, open and close their books, and shift positions. This will do away with any unnecessary movement or activity and will allow the group to relax. This process of relaxation will carry over into any appearance as a form of readiness.

The second principle is Concentration. The director who stresses the value of concentration and who insists upon this day after day, will develop professional poise and polish in each performance.

Set the stage for your rehearsals. This is a big step toward fostering concentration in the group. Choose a room that is quiet and uncrowded. Before the group arrives for rehearsal, set up the chairs, benches or stools. Close the window shades if possible, to shut out distracting sights and sounds. Be there, prepared, cool, calm, and pleasant. Create the proper atmosphere for concentration and ask the readers to help you by leaving outside all books, unfinished candy bars, coke bottles, chatter, and if possible, problems and worries.

The reader should concentrate first of all upon the book and his materials. Later, he can widen his circle of concentration to include the other readers and his own position in the group. The climax of public solitude comes when he can include the audience, its responses and reactions, in his circle of concentration, yet remain master of his own voice and body.

Active attention is absolutely essential. Irrelevant distractions or interruptions, divided attention and uneven concentration on the central task are all wasteful of time and energy. Your group must rehearse with a wide awake mind or they might better not be rehearsing at all. Tell them to experience and re-experience each time they read. Reading mechanically in practice cannot be effective preparation for communication. The reader must concentrate on thinking each thought completely, visualizing each image thoroughly, and upon recreating the image of each attitude and emotion intensely each time he reads aloud. Concentration causes images to file before the mind's eye; the same emotion will affect him, the same muscular reactions will flow through his body each time he reads. He will learn to concentrate until his inner feeling permeates.

We can hear the active and concentrating mind speaking. When reading becomes drab and mechanical, when a single reader is merely mouthing sounds, the other readers can sense it and fear for an imperfect reading. The audience knows too.

The third and perhaps most basic of the principles used in developing effective choric speech is Rhythm. Rhythm is a fundamental principle of the universe. Richard Boleslavsky, in his book *Acting: The First Six Lessons*, has said, "To exist is to have rhythm." The more complete our adjustment to the rhythm of life, the more harmonious, simple, and pleasant are our lives.

We see rhythm in the wash of the breakers on the beach, the seasonal flight of birds, the return of day and night, the cycle of the seasons, the phases of the moon. We hear it in music, we feel it in dance.

Psychologists say the basis of rhythm is within ourselves, our pulse, breathing, muscular movements, tension, and relaxation. All our pleasure comes from this. Rhythm is also a fundamental element in speech. The sound of words comes to its full power only through rhythm. In group speaking or in solo reading, the use of movement, pantomime, or dance, enhances the word images for both reader and audience.

32

Rhythm gives spirit and mood to the selection and makes the difference between mechanical rendition and fluency and interpretation.

The rhythm in poetry can usually be detected very easily. The poet often indicates in his title the intended rhythm. Take for example "Those Evening Bells" by Thomas Moore, "The Old Clock on the Stairs" by Longfellow, or "Sweet and Low" by Tennyson. Set up an ostinato of "ding dong," "tick tock," or "bye bye." The ostinato may be set up by using a guitar, bass fiddle or other musical instrument, or simply by beating on the books. You will find the poem emerging not sing-songy but in action phrases. You will not have to stress emphasis on certain words or pauses in designated places. The poet, the rhythm, the reader, have cooperated in interpreting the piece so that it catches the audience off guard and makes them glad.

When prose is beautiful it also becomes rhythmical. Rhythm in prose is suggested by the idea and arrangement of words. There is rhythm of content, which is established by the organization of the thought progression and the emotional progression. It depends upon the key words and phrases and on the major and minor climaxes throughout the selection.

There is also a rhythm in prose structure which becomes evident when it is read aloud. The prose rhythm is established by the length and grammatical construction of the sentences and phrases and by the position of the stresses. As the interpreter groups words into thought and action units he separates them by pauses, creating a cadence. A cadence is a flow of sound. Length and frequency of the pauses interrupting this flow of sound become a part of prose rhythm.

The readers will become sensitive to the natural rhythm in both prose and poetry and will use this to reinforce the total pleasing effect of the literature.

In other words we are saying that to do anything well, to create the greatest pleasure for our audience empathically, we must have educated our bodies, our neuromuscular machines, so that they show a pleasing rhythmical control. Develop a rhythm within your group with economy of force and coordinated timing. Precision in delivery will follow.

Relaxation, Concentration, and Rhythm then are the basic

principles in insuring the success of a speaking choir. Stressing these repeatedly will do away with the necessity of tedious drill upon phrasing, emphasis, inflection and pausing. Even diction and articulation will sharpen with the development of muscular control. Pleasing tone quality, variety, vitality and sparkle will result. Herein is the charm of group reading.

CHOREOGRAPHING THE PRODUCTION:
TECHNIQUES FOR THE ADVANCED CHOIR

"The words were spoken as if there were no book,
Except that the reader leaned above the page."

—Wallace Stevens

We have learned some of the basic principles involved in vitalizing choric speech. The next step is to organize a verse choir. We should observe some of the elements implied in this procedure.

The first necessary element is the leader. Qualifications for a good leader include personality, patience, imagination, leadership ability, and training. A careless, indifferent choir can evoke little empathy from an audience. Similarly a director who is not careful of personal appearance, or one with an unpleasant voice can alienate a choir. The leader should have, then, an attractive appearance and a good speaking voice. Further, he should possess abundant health and vitality.

One of the most important attributes for a director is patience. The training, especially with a newly organized choir, may be a slow process with results not always encouraging. Outbursts of temper or unkind criticism causes an unfavorable mounting of tension. These tensions will interfere with relaxation and concentration in the group and there will be no resulting "readiness."

Next, and equally important, the director should possess imagination. The leader of choral reading should be able to visualize the literature as implied action, to read between the lines, and to interpret carefully the author's attitude and intent. Furthermore, imagination will aid him in guiding the group to interesting and exciting interpretations. A good leader will encourage and make use of these group ideas if they are at all practical.

A choric choir requires organization. The director, therefore, should have leadership ability. When the director calls a rehearsal, he should be prepared, have the room set up and ready, materials ready for distribution, and a definite plan of action at his fingertips. Then he should proceed with enthusiasm and patience to direct the group, but never to dictate.

Finally, the director should have some training, not only in English and speech, but in music, dance, and dramatics. Some elements of staging, lighting, and costuming can be used to great advantage in a group, and music adds to the general effectiveness of any program.

The ideal leader will possess these personal and professional qualities and will also avail himself of every experience possible; travel, seeing good stage productions, and reading and studying good literature. This enrichment will inspire and challenge the members of the group.

Delegate duties to each member of your choir by selecting committees. There may be committees on materials, benches, music, transportation, and publicity. This will further the feeling of unity and oneness that a group of readers must possess.

Who should belong to a verse choir? How many members is ideal? Povenmire's study reveals that the number varies from ten or twelve to one hundred. Mary Gwen Owen, asks her students two questions only. They are: "Do you like to read?" and "Do you have time to read?" This is a great opportunity to use inexperienced and shy children, young people, or adults. Amount of talent, race and color shouldn't be criteria for choiring. Stutterers and those with other handicaps have become fluent readers when they read as a group. Regional differences are forgotten as each reader seeks to blend his voice into the rhythm of the group.

This author believes that from twenty-five to forty is ideal for a group. The choir may travel from one location to another to give programs. If the choir is too large, it is difficult and expensive to transport and also difficult to arrange on a small stage. Too many voices set up a resounding echo that distorts in an ordinary sized room.

Pleasing selections may be arranged with a few voices, but the danger is that the members fall into the category of Readers' Theatre or Chamber Theatre if the director does not take care. Whatever your number, choose your people with care to emphasize loyalty, dependability, and a desire to experience and understand good literature.

Your greatest problem may be the choosing and arranging of materials. You may be constantly on the lookout for new things, or you must discover the potentialities in old things. Not all good literature lends itself to multiple voices. Pieces with long sections of narration are too wordy and will not adapt themselves spontaneously, nor hold the attention of the group, nor of an audience. Some material is too intimate—some lends itself much better to solo inter-pretation.

Choose a theme and then find several numbers to fit this theme. Combine the reading with music, dance, and move-ment to enhance the literature. Keep your eyes open when you read *Newsweek*, *Life*, or *Saturday Review*. Many articles are adaptable to choric speaking and are exciting and contemporary. Several authors of books on group speaking have included lists of selections appropriate for a verse choir; but don't limit yourself to these. Search for your own. Ask your members to help your search. They will come up with some great ideas.

After you have chosen your materials, they must be typed, secured in a cover so that the script may be handled easily and skillfully. Half sheets of regulation typing paper are easier to handle than full sheets, and they are less apt to cover the faces of the readers when they are held for reading. Double type on each sheet with wide margins and do not include any markings or other instructions. Let the readers mark their own as they work together to interpret and create. Three-ring notebooks to fit the pages, with hard backs, are durable and convenient. These can be held in one hand, while the other hand turns pages, holds props, or parts of costumes required for the program. Corduroy covers fastened on as mother did to protect school books, adds to the attract-iveness of the book. Black corduroy covers may be slipped off easily and red ones slipped on, for a change of mood or atmosphere. These books become useful props and may be used in many ways to enhance the selections. Beat on the closed books to establish rhythm. Use great precision in opening and shutting the books. Take care in turning pages so that there is no rustle. Polish and precision is the secret for an effective performance.

Now the choir members have scripts in hand and are ready to mark the material, guided by the director. Each leader will, no doubt, develop his own system of marking. Horizontal lines between words indicate pauses; lines drawn beneath words are for emphasis. These can be used sparingly if the rhythm of the selection is established. Other instructions are written in the margins.

Strive for much variety in interpretation. Phrases should be of varying lengths in order to avoid monotony and a choppy effect. Do not divide the group into static groups as light, dark, medium, or soprano, alto, bass, tenor. Speaking voices do not necessarily fall into the same category as singing voices. Rather, choose voices that fit the meaning and tone of the lines to be read. Search for personalities whose voices picture the attitude and intent of the author, or of the character depicted by the author. Just as you cast a play, cast your people for effective and expressive interpretation of the selection. This will not be easy at first but experience will help. Again, listen to suggestions from your readers. Their ears are open and in tune. Never forget that the rhythm of the selection, poetry or prose, should be established first. Cadence, flow of sound, will follow.

Once the selection has been arranged and blocked, the leader may begin to withdraw. Various leaders in the group, placed in key positions where the others can see him, will effectively lead the group. When the numbers are ready for final rehearsal, the leader may fade away into the audience and enjoy a lively, delightful program. Your readers will relax, concentrate, keep their voices high and light, and each reader will be radiant with a smile and a warm aliveness.

Be imaginative in your arrangement of the group. Get away from the old singing choir formation. Bleachers do not allow for flexibility of movement. Levels of some sort can be used effectively. The Northwestern College group uses benches constructed by the young men in the group. Five-ply wood was cut in twelve by twelve, twelve by twenty-four, and twelve by thirty-six inch sizes. These benches will hold one, two, or three persons respectively. Phalanges at each corner hold the steel legs cut into three lengths. These screw in and out. On the bottom of each leg is a rubber tip. Later two sets of folding steps were added to the benches, and several step-ladders in various sizes. These were all painted black and they afford opportunity for many interesting formations and movement for different numbers. An added and great advantage is that the legs can be removed, the steps folded, and the entire set of seats can be placed in the trunk of a car for travel.

The material is in order, the group has been seated or stood in place. Now turn your attention toward using, music, dance, lighting, costuming or properties to enhance your presentation and to aid in the interpretation of the literature.

Guitars have been used successfully to establish the rhythm of a selection. This instrument is especially good with contemporary material. A bass-fiddle sets up a strong rhythmical beat. Humming or singing can be interspersed or combined with speaking parts.

Elaborate costuming is not necessary, but uniform dress adds much to the effectiveness of the group. Dark shirts and trousers with uniform blouses and shirts would be a good way to begin. The girls move more freely and gracefully if they wear long skirts. The hair line is important. Keep the hair away from the face. The girls may wear headbands to secure their hair. Remember facial expression and use of the eyes is an all important aid to interpretation.

Use bits of costuming, hats or colored scarves, to aid in characterization, especially in choric drama numbers. A few props may be used, although all of these devices should be used sparingly and intelligently. The literature will speak for itself to a great extent, if interpretation has been complete.

Lighting the faces of the readers helps the audience to focus its attention on them. A small control board and two standards holding ordinary floods and spots can be plugged into any 110 AC socket.

Very effective for some selections is the use of projections. The simplest method is to prepare transparenices and use an overhead projector, but 35 mm. slides in color are also good when projected on to a screen or gauze curtain. Projections are always somewhat distorted and unclear; you are not striving for reality. They do set the mood and illustrate graphically the thought of the selection.

Interpretative dance, usually by a solo dancer, blends beautifully with the spoken word. Several readers may form a group in front of the choir and use sustained movement or pantomime to add to the beauty of the words. The human body is a great interpreter. This body movement will be enhanced by using 3/8 inch dowel sticks, 36 inches long. Various figures and gestures may be formed with the sticks as crosses, stars, mangers, etc., or use them simply to point or emphasize.

A skillful blending of all of these fine arts will produce an artistic and thrilling production and will convince an audience that group reading is indeed a lively art.

SELECTIONS FOR THE YOUNG OF ALL AGES*

"The little ones leaped, and shouted, and laugh'd
And all the hills echoed."—William Blake

Preparation

Begin with light and simple poems—lullabies, humorous or activity poems such as "How Creatures Move" where the children can take turns at being the animals and moving to the rhythm of the words. Or make use of action poems in which part of the group tells the poem and part engages in the action. For example, in such a poem as "The Cat" have the children suggest bodily movement to emphasize the rhythm and help them to appreciate the idea of the poem. Good activity poems will naturally lead to poems with choral refrains. Here the teacher will begin by saying the stanza, with the group saying the refrain; later the stanza may be

---

*This introduction was written by Dr. Arthur T. Allen, (deceased) Department of Education and English, Brooklyn College of the City University of New York. The selections in this group were chosen by him.

assigned to one group and the refrain to another. Try arranging your selections in different ways. Perhaps the children can think of other ways to say the poem.

Line-a-child is a sequential arrangement in which each line is spoken by a different child with a "building-up" to the climactic line or lines which are spoken by the entire group. In contrast, there is the antiphonal type of group reading which is essentially two part arrangements where two contrasting voice groups speak alternate lines or verses of a poem.

Finally, there is the unison or voice group with added variations of arrangements. In the unison approach the entire choral speaking group recites together as if with one voice; whereas in voice group parts complementary voices in various group and solo arrangements are employed to achieve a creatively synchronized interpretation of the poem. By far these types are the most difficult.

With today's children, it is difficult to come up with "closely graded poetry" as was the approach years ago. Some of the following poems have been used with "children" from ages 6 to 60. The teacher's common sense and know-how in working with children are the best criteria for determining which poem(s) will possibly "turn-on" or "turn-off" his pupils. It appears that children are desirous of the more challenging material and move quickly in their abilities from the simple ditty to the more expressive poem where concentration is required to communicate the thought.

Reading poetry together is essentially for enjoyment, not for demonstration; it is a group activity for children to engage in in the classroom. But there are times when children might want to share the beauty that they have created with other children, and with cooperative leadership from the teacher and the group a special program might be arranged and it, too, can become a creative outlet for all who become involved.

SELECTIONS FOR THE YOUNG OF ALL AGES

SECTION 1—*Activity Poems*

HOW CREATURES MOVE

The lion walks on padded paws
The squirrel leaps from limb to limb,
While flies crawl straight up a wall
And seals can dive and swim.
The worm he wiggles all around
The monkey swings by his tail
And birds may hop upon the ground
Or spread their wings and sail.
But boys and girls
Have much more fun;
They leap and dance
And walk and run.

Unknown

CAT*

The black cat yawns.
Opens her jaws,
Stretches her legs,
And shows her claws.

Then she gets up
And stands on four
Long stiff legs
And yawns some more.

She shows her sharp teeth,
She stretches her lip,
Her slice of a tongue
Turns up at the tip.

*"Cat" by Mary B. Miller. ©Copyright, Estate of Mary B. Miller. Reprinted with permission.

Lifting herself
On her delicate toes,
She arches her back
As high as it goes.

She lets herself down
With particular care,
And pads away
With her tail in the air.

Mary Britton Miller

Walk around the room and express the actions openly and
freely. Excellent for relaxation at the beginning of a group
reading session.

AUTUMN MOOD*

A golden leaf is falling to the ground. . . .
Hush!. . . . . . . Hush!
With just the faintest whisper of a sound. . . .
Brush!. . . . . .Brush!
Leaves
   and leaves,
   and swirling in a shower. . . .
   Still!. . . . . . Still!
A golden rain is falling on the hill.

Louise Abney

Dance movement and background recorded music could be
employed.

*From *Choral Speaking Arrangements for
the Upper grades*
by Louise Abney. © 1937
Expression Co.

43

GRASSHOPPER GREEN*

Grasshopper Green is a comical chap;
He lives on the best of fare.
Bright little trousers, jacket and cap,
These are his summer wear.
Out in the meadows he loves to go,
Playing away in the sun;
It's hopperty, skipperty, high and low—
Summer's the time for fun.

Grasshopper Green has a dozen wee boys,
And soon as their legs grow strong,
Each of them joins in his frolicsome joys,
Singing his merry song.
Under the hedge in a happy row
Soon as the day has begun,
It's hopperty, skipperty, high and low—
Summer's the time for fun.

Grasshopper Green has a quaint little house.
It's under the hedge so gay.
Grandmother Spider, as still as a mouse,
Watches him over the way.
Gladly he's calling the children, I know,
Out in the beautiful sun;
It's hopperty, skipperty, high and low—
Summer's the time for fun.

Unknown

*From *Choral Speaking for Speech Improvement*
by Carrie Rasmussen.
© 1953 Expression Co.

THE BIG BLACK CLOCK*

Slowly ticks the big clock;
Tick-tock, tick-tock!
But Cuckoo Clock ticks a double quick:
Tick-a-tocka, tick-a-tocka,
Tick-a-tocka, tick!

THE MILK MAN'S HORSE

One summer morning when it's hot,
The milkman's horse can't even trot,
But pokes along this this—
Klip-klop, klip-klop, klip-klop.

But in the winter brisk,
He perks right up and wants to frisk,
and then he goes like this—
Klipity-klop, klipity-klop, klipity-klop.
Klipity, klipity, klop.

Unknown

"The Big Black Clock"
"The Milkman's Horse" pp. 23,24.
*"From *The Sound of Poetry,*"
Austln, Mary C. and Queenie B. Mills, eds.
Allyn and Bacon.©1963.

WELL, I NEVER?

Two little mice went tripping down the street,
      Pum catta-pum chin chin,
One wore a bonnet and a green silk shirt,
One wore trousers and a nice clean shirt;
      Pum catta-pum chin chin.
One little hen went tripping down the street,
      Pum catta-pum chin chin.
One little hen very smart and spry,
With a wig-wagging tail and a wicked little eye,
      Pum catta-pum chin chin.

Rose Fyleman

WE THANK THEE

For flowers so beautiful and sweet,
For friends and clothes and food to eat,
For precious hours, for work and play,
We thank Thee this Thanksgiving Day.

For father's care and mother's love,
For the blue sky and clouds above,
For springtime and for autumn gay,
We thank Thee this Thanksgiving Day.

For all Thy gifts so good and fair,
Bestowed so freely everywhere,
Give us grateful hearts we pray,
To thank Thee this Thanksgiving Day.

Unknown

Teacher or a superior reader should read the solo parts; children can repeat the refrain "We thank Thee this Thanksgiving Day."

"Well, I Never?" from *The Faber Book of Children's Verse*, reprinted by permission of Faber and Faber Ltd.

THE SWAPPING SONG*

My father he died, but I never knew how.
He left me six horses to drive in my plow,
   With a wim, wam, waddle-o
   Stick, stock, straddle-o,
   Fin, fan, faddle-o
   All the way home.
I sold my six horses and bought me a cow
To make me a fortune but I didn't know how.
   With a wim, wam, etc.
I sold my cow and bought me a calf,
And in that trade I lost just half.
   With a wim, wam, etc.
I sold my calf and bought me a mule,
And then I rode like a gol-darned fool.
   With a wim, wam, etc.
I sold my mule and swapped for it for a pig;
It wouldn't grow much and it wasn't very big
   With a wim, wam, etc.
I sold my pig and bought me a cat;
The pretty little creature in the corner sat.
      With a wim, wam, etc.
I sold my cat and bought me a mouse;
His tail caught fire and burned down the house.
      With a wim, wam, waddle-o,
      Stick, stock, straddle-o
      Fin, fan, faddle-o,
      All the way home.

                    Kentucky Mountain Song

Excellent for rhythm, diction and articulation. Employ the
guitar as an accompaniment. Make the rhythm obvious.

*From *Rainbow in the Sky*, Louis Untermeyer,
ed., Copyright 1935 by Harcourt Brace Jovanovich, Inc.
Reprinted by permission of the publisher.

PIPPA'S SONG

The year's at the spring
And day's at the morn;
Morning's at seven;
The hillside's dew-pearled;
The lark's on the wing:
The snail's on the thorn;
God's in his heaven—
All's right with the world.

Robert Browning

Each child speaks a line and dances as she speaks. The seated group speaks the last line. Musical accompaniment suggested.

BOW, WOW, SAYS THE DOG*

Bow, wow, says the dog;
Mew, mew, says the cat;
Grunt, grunt, says the pig;
And squeak, says the rat;
Tu, whu, says the owl;
Caw, caw, goes the crow;
Quack, quack, goes the duck;
And moo, moo, says the cow.

Mother Goose

*From *The Oxford Nursery Rhyme Book* Reprinted by permission of the Oxford University Press © 1955.

MONDAY'S CHILD

Monday's child is fair of face
Tuesday's child if full of grace
Wednesday's child if full of woe
Thurday's child has far to go
Friday's child is loving and giving
Saturday's child works hard for a living.
But the child that's born on Sunday
Will be bonny and good and gay.

Mother Goose

COMPARISONS

As wet as a fish—as dry as a bone;
As live as a bird—as dead as a stone;
As plump as a partridge—as poor as a rat;
As strong as a horse—as weak as a cat;
As hard as a flint—as soft as a mole;
As white as a lily—as black as coal;
As plain as a staff—as rough as a bear;
As light as a drum—as free as the air;
As heavy as lead—as light as a feather;
As steady as time—as uncertain as weather;
As hot as an oven—as cold as a frog;
As gay as a lark—as sick as a dog;
As savage as tigers—as mild as a dove;
As stiff as a poker—as limp as a glove;
As blind as a bat as deaf as a post;
As cool as a cucumber—as warm as toast;
As flat as a flounder—as round as a ball;
As blunt as a hammer—as sharp as an owl;
As brittle as glass—as tough as gristle;
As red as a rose—as square as a box;
As bold as a thief—as sly as a fox.

Unknown

*From *The Oxford Nursery Rhyme Book*.
Opic, Jona and Peter Opic Comps.
Reprinted by permission of the Oxford Univ. Press.
©1955.

Possibly children could add other lines. Pantomime or individual art work could be employed.

WHAT IS PINK?

What is pink?
   a rose is pink
By the fountain's brink.
What is red?
   a poppy's red
In its barley bed.
What is blue?
   The sky is blue
Where the clouds float through.
What is white?
   A swan is white
Sailing in the light.
What is yellow?
   Pears are yellow
Rich and ripe and mellow.
What is green?
   The grass is green
With flowers in between.
What is violet?
   Clouds are violet
In the summer twilight.
What is orange?
   Why an orange is orange,
Just an orange!

Christina Rosetti

WINTER

Don't you like winter, though!
The white of it,
the might of it,
the squinty, glinty sight of it,
the strange blue light of it,
the stars each early night of it!

Glare of ice.
Air like spice.
Don't you like snow!
The swirl of it,
the twirl of it,
the busy windy whirl of it;
creaky, squeaky frozen snow,
streaky hills where skiers go,
quiet starry flakes that fall,
purple snow where shadows sprawl,
the space and all.

Don't you like winter, though,
    and snow!

Aileen Fisher

Combine music, and dance, and use projection of a winter
scene to enhance the selection.

SECTION 3—*Antiphonal*

LAUGHTER

The North Wind laughs with a loud Ho! Ho!
The South Wind laughs with a Whee!
The snowman laughs at the swirling snow
And some folks laugh at *me!*

Fairies laugh with a twinkling laugh
Which sounds like a fairy bell.
And goblins snicker and laugh He! He!
At the secrets which goblins tell.
When the little Easter bunny laughs,
He wrinkles up his nose;
And the clown in the circus laughs out loud
As round the ring he goes.

Unknown

51

PUSSY AND THE MICE

"Pussy and the Mice" from *The Moon is Shining Bright as Day* Reprinted by permission of Curtis Brown Ltd. Copyright 1953, by Ogden Nash.

Three little mice sat down to spin,
Pussy passed by and she looked in.
"What are you doing, my little men?"
"We're making coats for gentlemen."
"Shall I come in and bite off your threads?"
"No, no, Miss Pussy, you'll bite off our heads."
"Oh, no, I'll not. I'll help you spin"
"That may be so, but you don't come in."

Unknown

WHISTLE, MAMIE

Whistle, Mamie, whistle;
I'll give you a cow.
I can't whistle;
I don't know how.
Whistle, Mamie, whistle;
I'll give you a pig.
I can't whistle,
I'm too big.

Whistle, Mamie, whistle,
I'll give you a man.
I can't—Whee!—
Yes, I guess I can!

Unknown

SECTION 4—*Unison or Voice Group Parts*

ELETELEPHONY

Once there was an elephant,
   Who tried to use the telephant—/
No! No! I mean an elephone

Who tried to use the telephone—/(sigh)/
(Dear me! I am not certain quite
    That even now I've got it right.)
How e'er it was, he got his trunk,
    Entangled in the elephunk;/
The more he tried to get it free,
    The louder buzzed the telephee—/
Slow   (I fear I'd better drop the song
        of elephop and telephong!)

Laura E. Richards

Pause markings are essential!

LINDA'S LOCKET

Little Linda lost her locket,
Lovely, lucky, little locket,
Little Linda found her locket
Lying still in Linda's pocket.

Unknown

*The heavens are telling the glory of God; and the firmament proclaims His handiwork. Day to day pours forth speech, and night to night declares knowledge. There is no speech, nor are there words; their voice is not heard; yet their voice goes forth through all the earth; and their words to the end of the world.

Psalm 19 RSV

AFRICAN DANCE

The low beating of the tom-toms,
The slow beating of the tom-toms,
    Low. . .slow
    Slow. . .low—
Stirs your blood.

Dance!
A night-veiled girl
  Whirls softly into a
  Circle of light
Whirls softly. . .slowly,
Like a wisp of smoke around the fire.
  And the tom-toms beat,
  And the tom-toms beat,
And the low beating of the tom-toms
  Stirs your blood.

Langston Hughes

Use a bongo to set up an ostinato. Stick firmly to the beat.
Dance might be employed in the second stanza.

LISTEN TO THE RAIN

Pitter, patter, pitter, patter
Listen to the rain,
Splish, splash, splish, splash,
On the window pane.

Tap, tap, tap, tap,
Dancing on the leaves,
Drip, drip, drip, drip,
Falling from the eaves.

Tap, tap, splish, splash
Then drip, drip again. . . .
Pitter, pitter, patter, don't you
Like to hear it rain?

Marion Kennedy

Use simple rhythm instruments for accompaniment.

THANKFULNESS

Make a joyful noise unto the Lord, all ye lands./
Serve the Lord with gladness;/ come before
    His presence with singing!
Know ye that the Lord He is God:/ it is He that
    hath made us, and not we ourselves;/
    we are His people, and the sheep of His
    pasture./
Enter into His gates with thanksgiving,
    and unto His courts with praises:/
    be thankful unto Him,/ and bless His name./
For the Lord is good;/ His mercy is everlasting;
    and His truth endureth to all generations./

The Bible: Psalm 100

Music has been written for this selection. Male quartet could
follow the reading.

THE MYSTERIOUS CAT*

I saw a proud, mysterious cat
I saw a proud, mysterious cat
Too proud to catch a mouse or rat—
Mew, mew, mew.
But catnip she would eat, and purr,
But catnip she would eat, and purr.
And goldfish she did much perfer—
Mew, mew, mew.

I saw a cat—'twas but a dream,
I saw a cat—'twas but a dream.
Who scorned the slave that brought her cream—
Mew, mew, mew.

*Reprinted with permission of Macmillan
Publishing Co., Inc., from Collected Poems
by Vachel Lindsay.
©1941 by Macmillan Co., Inc.
Renew 1942 by Elizabeth C. Lindsay.

Unless the slave were dressed in style,
Unless the slave were dressed in style
And knelt before her all the while—
Mew, mew, mew.

Did you ever hear of a thing like that?
Did you ever hear of a thing like that?
Did you ever hear of a thing like that?
Oh, what a proud mysterious cat.
Oh, what a proud mysterious cat.
Mew. . .Mew. . .Mew. . .

Vachel Lindsay

THE FROG

What a wonderful bird the frog are:
When he stand, he sit—almost;
Whe he hop, he fly—almost.
He ain't got no sense hardly,
He ain't got no tail hardly either.
When he sit, he sit on what he ain't got—almost.

Unknown

Girls read in unison keeping voices high and light. Boys' deep
voices can repeat the "almost."

"The Frog" from *The Man is Shining
Bright as Day*. ©1953 by Ogden Nash.
Reprinted by permission of Curtis Brown, Ltd.

COME AGAIN

Summer sunshine,
Autumn gold,
Blessed Christmas,
Bright and cold;
Flowers that follow
April rain,
Good-bye all, but
Come again—
Oh, come again!

Mary A. Lathbury

The above selection is suggested as a good closing for a program of group reading.

SELECTIONS FOR FUN AND RHYTHM

The following selections can be used to develop a feeling of rhythm in the group. I have stressed rhythm as a basic element in interpretation and performance. There is much opportunity also to integrate music, dance, bits of costuming and a few properties.

The pauses are indicated by horizontal lines. Other instructions are given.

JAZZ FANTASIA*

(a poem illustrating change of rhythm)

men   *low women*   *high*
Drum on your drums,/batter on your banjos,/ sob

women   *Chorus*
on the long/cool/winding saxophones./Go to it,/

O   Jazzmen./

*Reprinted with permission of Harcourt
Brace Jovanovich. ©1962, from *Modern American
Poetry*, Louis Untermeyer, ed.

57

Sling your knuckles on the bottom of the happy

beat time
on books

(oooooo z)

Chorus   tin pans,/ let your trombones ooze, and go husha—

husha-hush with the slippery sandpaper./

(moooan) lean to left

Women   Moan like an autumn wind high in the lonesome

lean to right

tree tops,/ moan soft like you wanted

sit up

somebody terrible,/cry like a racing car
slipping away from a motorcycle cop,/

Chorus   bang-bang,/you jazzmen,/bang altogether

men   men   women   women

drums,/ traps,/ banjos,/ horns,/ tin cans/—make

two people fight on the top of a stairway
and scratch each other's eyes in a clinch
tumbling down the stairs./

fast, lean far
toward the floor

men   women

Can the rough stuff/. . . .Now a Mississippi
Steamboat pushes up the night river/with a

very soft
and sweet

sing,repeat

hoo-hoo-hoo-ooo. . .and the green lanterns
calling to the high soft stars/. . . .a red moon
rides on the humps of the low river

chorus

hills/. . . .Go to it, O jazzmen./

Carl Sandburg

For "Jazz Fantasia" it is best to have a leader stand in
front and face the group, and go through the action, or have
several leaders, one for each new rhythm.

58

NO

No sun—No moon—
No morn—no noon—
no dawn—no dusk—no proper time of day—
no sky—no earthly view—
no distant looking blue—
no road—no street—no "other side the way"—
no end to any row—
no indications where the crescents go—
no top to any steeple—
no recognitions of familiar people—
no courtesies for showing 'em—
No knowing 'em—

Chorus   no travelling at all—no locomotion
no inkling of the way—no notion—
"No go" by land or ocean—
no mail—no post—
no news from any foreign coast—
no park—no ring—no afternoon gentility—
no company—no nobility—
no warmth—no cheerfulness—no healthful ease—
no comfortable feel in any member—
no shade—no shine—no butterflies—no bees—
no fruits—no flowers—no leaves—no trees—

Chorus   November!
(softly)

Thomas Hood

November is a good example of the effectiveness of adding and subtracting voices. Assign each phrase to an individual or to a small group. As each recites, he or the group stand, until all are standing and reading together "no knowing 'em." Then the groups drop off and sit down in the same order as the upward build, Finally, all voices in unison come in in a whisper on the final "November." Try it!

THE SONG OF KERAMOS*

Chorus	Turn, turn, my wheel! Turn round and round Without a pause, without a sound; So spins the flying world away!
Solo 1	So spins the world away
Chorus	This clay, well mixed with marl and sand, Follows the motion of my hand; For some must follow, and some command, Though all are made of clay!
Solo 1	Turn, Turn, my wheel! All things must change To something new, to something strange; Nothing that is can pause or stay:
Chorus	Nothing can pause or stay
Solo 1	The moon will wax, the moon will wane, The mist and cloud will turn to rain, The rain to mist and cloud again, Tomorrow be today.
Chorus	Turn, turn, my wheel! All life is brief; What now is bud will soon be leaf, What now is leaf will soon decay;
Solo 1	The leaf will soon decay
Chorus	The wind blows east, the wind blows west; The blue eggs in the robin's nest Will soon have wings and beak and breast, And flutter and fly away.
Solo 2	Turn, turn, my wheel! This earthen jar A touch can make, a touch can mar; And shall it to the Potter say,
Chorus	And to the potter say
Solo 2	What makest thou? Thou has no hand? As men who think to understand A world by their Creator planned, Who wiser is than they.

*Reprinted by permission of Houghton,
Mifflin and Co. ©1893. From the *Complete
Works of Henry Longfellow.*

Chorus	Turn, turn, my wheel! 'Tis nature's plan
	The child should grow into the man,
	The man grow wrinkled, old, and gray
Solo 3	Grow wrinkled, old, and gray
Chorus	In youth the heart exults and sings,
	The pulses leap, the feet have wings!
	In age the cricket chirps, and brings
	The harvest of the day.
Solo	Turn, turn, my wheel! The human race,
	Of every tongue, of every place,
	Caucasian, Costic, or Malay.
Chorus	Roman or Pompeii
Solo 3	All that inhabit this great earth,
	Whatever be their rank or worth,
	Are kindred and allied by birth,
	And made of the same clay.
Chorus	Turn, turn, my wheel! What is begun
	At daybreak must at dark be done.
	Tomorrow will be another day;
Solo 4	Will be another day
Chorus	Tomorrow the hot furnace flame
	will search the heart and try the frame,
	And stamp with honor or with shame
	These vessels made of clay.
Solo 4	Stop, stop, my wheel! Too soon, too soon
	The noon will be the afternoon,
	Too soon today be yesterday;
Chorus	Today be yesterday
Solo 4	Behind us in our path we cast
	The broken potsherds of the past,
	And all are ground to dust at last,
	And trodden into clay.

Henry W. Longfellow

"Keramos" is a delightful selection. Set up the rhythm of the wheel turning and follow it throughout. There are no pauses excepting short ones taken when needed for breath. This is excellent for breath control. Keep the wheel turning! Use a guitar accompaniment, or better still, several guitars.

61

RACHEL MY OWN*

3 boys The first time that I saw my love,
     she was dressed in a gingham gown.
     I was just a stranger ridin' into town.
     Her hair was brighter than the sun,
     her smile was warm and gay.
     Her eyes looked up to greet my own,
     then shyly glanced away.

Chorus Rachel, Rachel, Rachel, my own.
     My heart will have no other,
     though the world I may roam.
     Rachel, Rachel, Rachel, my fair.
     If I could be beside you,
     I'd never stray from there.

3 boys The next time that I saw my love,
     she wore a wedding gown.
     She had wed another
     as I rode back to town.
     She had found another love,
     for me she could not wait.
     Oh, Rachel, did your heart not know
     that I'd return too late?

Chorus Rachel, Rachel, Rachel, my own.
     My heart will have no other,
     though the world I may roam.
     Rachel, Rachel, Rachel, my fair,
     If I could be beside you,
     I'd never stray from there.

Words by Arch and Jean Lustberg. Music by John Cacavas © 1965 by Carl Fischer, Inc., New York. International Copyright Secured. All Rights Reserved. Reprinted by permission of the publisher.

3 boys   The next time that I saw my love,
she wore a scarlet gown,
He left her for another
When he brought her down.
Oh, Rachel, love, I swear to you,
he'll pay for your disgrace.
I'll search the world over and
I'll kill him face to face.

Chorus   Rachel, Rachel, Rachel, my own.
My heart will have no other
though the world I may roam.
Rachel, Rachel, Rachel, my fair.
If I could be beside you,
I'd never stray from there.

3 boys   The last time that I saw my love
she wore a winding sheet.
They bore her on the road
beneath my dangling feet.
Her heart was faithful to the end,
I thought to shoot him dead,
But she threw herself before him,
and I killed my love instead.

Chorus   Rachel, Rachel, Rachel, my own.
My heart would have no other
Though the world I did roam.
Rachel, Rachel, Rachel, my fair.
They laid me down beside you.
I'll never stray from there.

(slow)   They laid me down beside you,
I'll never stray from there.

Arch and Jean Anne Lustberg

"Rachel My Own" is an old ballad, set to music. It is found on Pembroke Record No. CFM 2000 B, The John Cacavas Singers. Your choir will enjoy this melodrama. Speak it with guitar accompaniment, but catch the best from the music.

LIKE AN EAGLE*
by Lan O'Kun

Chorus   Like an Eagle flying in the sun
I fly free of sorrow/
Like the deer running on the plain
I run to tomorrow—I run to tomorrow./
The wind is a friend of mine,/
it blows where I go
Making my spirit light as the snow./
Like the minnow swimming in the stream
Endlessly I play/
Sleeping under stars and sky,
happy every day./
Like the river flowing from the past
or the rainwashed swallows,/
I've no bond that's holding me fast
and no road to follow,/
And no road to follow./
Like An Eagle, (cont.)
Time has no hand on me,/
and I've no special place,/
No angry spirit summons my face./
Like the willow weeping for the moon
so in life I sway/
dancing to a piper's tune
then going my own way/
forever going my own way./

Please do use interpretative dance with this number. Ask your reader to *accompany the dancer.* Music may be secured from Carl Fischer, Inc.

KEY LARGO

Chorus: As Main go o so pogo Key Largo
Otsego to Frisco go to Fargo
Okeefenokee playing Possum on a Pogo
Stick around and see the show
Go over landalive a band o jive will blow go Pogo
I go you go who go to go Polly voo go
From Caravan Diego, Waco and Oswego,
Tweedle de he go she go we go me go Pago

Girls: Atascadero Wheeler Barrow
Some Place in Mexico

Boys: Delaware Ohio and you
Don't need the text to go

Chorus: Wheeling, West Virginia
With everything that's in ya,
Down the line—You'll see the shine
From Oregon to Caroline.
Oh, eenie meenie minie Kokomo go Pogo
Tishimingo, sing those lingo, whistling go.

Shamoakin to Hoboken
Chenango to Chicongo
It's golly, I go googoo going go go Poga.

A study in rhythm and diction. Bodies should move also,
fingers snap, or whatever accentuates rhythm. Good luck!

THE MACHINE YES THE MACHINE*

The machine,/ yes,/ the machine
Never wastes/ anybody's time/
Never watches the foreman/
Never talks back/
Never says what is right or wrong/
The machine/ yes/ the machine/
Cuts your production costs/
A man is a man and what can you do with him?
A man is a man and what can you do with him?
But—
A machine—
Now you take—
A machine—
No kids—
No woman—
Never hungry—
Never thirsty—
All—
A machine needs—
Is a little/ reg/ular/ atte/ntion/—
And plenty—
of grease—   *run down*
And plenty—   *like a*
of grease—   *machine*
And plenty—
of grease—

Carl Sandburg

Keep the rhythm steady. Expressionless faces as a machine—
eyes unseeing—bodies may jerk to the rhythm. Use two short
pieces of steel pipe and an ordinary kitchen grater with a
metal scraper to accentuate the rhythm.

*From *The World of Carl Sandburg: A Stage Presentation* by
Norman Corwin, © 1960,1961 by Carl Sandburg. Reprinted
by permission of Harcourt, Brace Jovanovich, Inc.

THE TRAIN
by Keith Frolkey
(Northwestern College Student)

I see the road stretching
And crawling up the silent mountain slopes/
Moving rock and forest as she winds
Her tenuous fingers,/
Threatening ever to sever the life
From the mountain,/
Now cutting/
Dipping/,
Digging/,
Blocking/,
Shoveling and tunneling,/
As she gathers the flesh of the mountain
And disperses it throughout the valleys
And the crevices of the lower slopes/.
The road creeps on toward the cities/
     Of/
        MAN. . . . . .

faster   The road enters the plains,/
speed up It springs forward with an uncanny burst of speed:
Swallowing Denver,
Cheyenne,
And Omaha./
With a flood of concrete and asphalt,
It reaches Iowa and spreads out into
Symmetric cells of existence./
It rushes through Sioux City,
Des Moines,
Burlington,
And Dubuque;/
Rushing through Ohio,
Virginia,
And Pennsylvania;/
Running past Trenton,
Albany,
And Boston./

slower   She slows speed and as she does/
softly   She see the rocks and rills of home,
And silently/
She creeps up the mountain slopes
Releasing men from isolation/.
And carrying them toward the cities/
     Of/
         Man. . . ./
This is:/

THE TRAIN

THE MUSICAL TRUST
D.K. Stevens

(If possible, use instruments as indicated)

Chorus   There once was a man who could execute
"old Raccoon" on a yellow flute,/
And several other tunes to boot,/
flute   But he couldn't make a penny with his
       tootle-ti-toot/
Tootle-ootle-ootle tootle-ti-toot/
Tootle-ootle-ootle—tootle-ti-toot/.
Though he played all day on his yellow flute/,
He couldn't make a penny with his tootle-ti-toot./

Chorus   One day he met a singular (Sing-u-lar)
Quaint old man with a big tuba/
       Solo
Who said: "I've traveled wide and far
But I haven't made a penny with my oom-pah-pah"/
tuba   Oom-pah   Oom-pah   Oom-pah pah
Chorus   Oom-pah   Oom-pah   Oom-pah pah
Though he played all day on his big tuba/.
He couldn't make a penny with him oom-pah-pah/.

Chorus	They met two men who were hammering/ On a big bass drum and a Cymbal thing,/ Who said: "We've banged since early spring, (2 men) And we haven't made a penny with our boom-zing-zing
Chorus drum cymbal	Boom-zing Boom-zing Boom-zing-zing Boom-b-b-boom-boom—zing-zing Though they banged on the drum and the cymbal thing/ They couldn't make a penny with their boom-zing-zing/.

flute

Chorus	So the man with the flute played tootle-ti-toot/,

tuba

And the other man played oom-pah-pah/
While the man with the drum and the cymbal thing

     drum   *cymbal*

Went: Boom-b-b-boom-boom—zing-zing. And they
traveled wide and far/. Together they made the

     flute   *tuba*

Welkin ring./ With a Tootle-ootle Oom-pah

drum   *cymbal*   *flute*   *tuba*   *drum*

Boom-zing-zing. Tootle-ootle Oom-pah Boom-zing-zing
And Oh, the pennies the people fling!?
When they hear the tootle-oom-pah-boom-zing-zing!

"Night Mail" by W.H. Auden also has a marked rhythm. As
you can guess, the rhythm is that of a moving train. While the
women read the first section, the men "choo choo" the
sound of the engine. This ostinato establishes your beat.

Programs With a Theme

Interesting and unusual programs may be planned using a
theme, then finding several poems to carry out the theme.
This group of selections presents some ideas. You will be able
to think of others, perhaps more suited to your needs.

The poems in this group should be recited by male voices, using solo voices or a group. A picture frame could be built and each girl could pose in the frame during the recitation of the poem.

You will notice that some of these poems have been set to music. Others suggest musical numbers. Use this music as background, or let a quartet of boys sing between the numbers. Hats, bits of costuming, and various groupings will add much to the effectiveness of your presentation.

MAID OF ATHENS, ERE WE PART

Maid of Athens, ere we part,
Give, oh give me back my heart;
Or, since that has left my breast
Keep it now, and take the rest
Hear my vow before I go,

By those tresses unconfined,
Woo'd by each Aegean wind;
By those lids whose jetty fringe
Kiss thy soft cheeks' blooming tinge;
By those wild eyes like the roe,
By that lip I long to taste;
By that zone-encircled waist;
By all the token-flowers that tell
What words can never speak so well;
By love's alternate joy and woe.

Maid of Athens! I am gone:
Think of me, sweet! When alone.
Though I fly to Istanbul,
Athens holds my heart and soul;
Can I cease to love thee? No!

Lord Byron

SONG TO CELIA

Drink to me only with thine eyes,
   And I will pledge with mine;
Or leave a kiss but in the cup,
   And I'll not look for wine.
The thirst that from the soul doth rise
   Doth ask a drink divine;
But might I of Jove's nectar sup,
   I would not change for thine.

I sent thee late a rosy wreath,
   Not so much honoring thee
As giving it a hope, that there
   It could not withered be,
But thou thereon didst only breathe,
   And sent'st it back to me;
Since when it grows, and smells, I swear,
   Not of itself, but thee.

                          Ben Jonson

WHO IS SYLVIA

Who is Sylvia? What is she,
   That all our swains commend her?
Holy, fair, and wise is she;
   That heaven such grace did lend her,
That she might admired be.

Is she kind as she is fair?
   For beauty lives with kindness.
Love doth to her eyes repair,
   To help him of his blindness,
And, being helped, inhabits there.

Then to Sylvia let us sing,
   That Sylvia is excelling:
She excels each mortal thing
   Upon the dull earth dwelling;
To her let us garlands bring.

William Shakespeare

JENNY KISS'D ME

Jenny kissed me when we met.
Jumping from the chair she sat in.
Time, you thief: who love to get
Sweets into your list, put that in.
Say I'm weary, say I'm sad;
Say that health and wealth have missed me;
Say I'm growing old, but add—
Jenny kissed me.

James Henry Leigh Hunt

NANCY HANKS*

"You wouldn't know
About my son?
Did he grow tall?
Did he have fun?
Did he learn to read?
Did he get to town?
Do you know his name?
Did he get on?"

A reply to Nancy Hanks

Yes, Nancy Hanks,
The news we will tell
Of your Abe
Whom you loved so well.
You asked first,
"Where's my son?"
He lives in the *heart*
of *everyone.*

Rosemary Benet and
Stephen Vincent Benet

JEANIE WITH THE LIGHT BROWN HAIR*

I dream of Jeanie with the light brown hair,
Borne, like a vapor, on the summer air;
I see her tripping where the bright streams play,
Happy as the daisies that dance on her way.
Many were the wild notes her merry voice would pour,
Many were the blithe birds that warbled them o'er;
Oh! I dream of Jeanie with the light brown hair,
Floating, like a vapor, on the summer air.

*From: *A Book of Americans* by Rosemary and Stephen Vincent
Benet. Holt, Rhinehart and Winston, Inc. Copyright 1933 by Rosemary
and Stephen Vincent Benet. Copyright renewed © by Rosemary Carr
Benet. Reprinted by permission of Brandt and Brandt.

*Reprinted by permission of Grosset and Dunlap, Inc.

I long for Jeanie with the day-dawn smile,
Radiant in gladness, warm with winning guile;
I hear her melodies, like joys gone by,
sighing round my heart o'er the fond hopes that die.
Sighing like the wind and sobbing like the rain,
Wailing for the lost one that comes not again:
Oh! I long for Jeanie, and my heart bows low,
Never more to find her where the bright waters flow.

Stephen Foster

LITTLE ANNIE ROONEY

A winning way, a pleasant smile,
Dress'd so neat but quite in style,
Merry chaff your time to while,
Has little Annie Rooney;
Ev'ry ev'ning, rain or shine,
I make a call twixt eight and nine,
On her who shortly will be mine,
Little Annie Rooney.

She's my sweetheart, I'm her beau,
She's my Annie, I'm her Joe.
Soon we'll marry, never to part,
Little Annie Rooney is my sweetheart.

The parlor's small but neat and clean,
And set with taste so seldom seen,
And you can bet the household queen
Is little Annie Rooney!
The fire burns cheerfully and bright,
As a family circle round, each night
We form and every one's delight
Is little Annie Rooney.

We've been engaged close on a year,
The happy time is drawing near
I'll wed the one I love so dear
Little Annie Rooney.
My friends declare I am in jest
Until the time comes will I rest
But one who knows its value best
Is Little Annie Rooney.

When married we'll so happy be
I love her and she loves me
Happier wife you'll never see
Than Little Annie Rooney.

In a little cozy home,
No more from her I'll care to roam.
She'll greet you all whenever you come
My Little Annie Rooney.

Michael Nolan

PROVERBS 31*

vs. 10-31

A good wife who can find?
She is far more precious than jewels.
The heart of her husband trusts in her,
    and he will have no lack of gain.
She does him good, and not harm, all the days of her life.
She seeks wool and flax, and works with willing hands.
She is like the ships of the merchant, she brings her
    food from afar.
She rises while it is yet night and provides food for
    her household, and tasks for her maidens.
She considers a field and buys it;
    With the fruit of her hands she plants a vineyard.
She girds her loins with strength and makes her arms strong.
She perceives that her merchandise is profitable.

Her lamp does not go out at night.
She puts her hands to the distaff, and her hands hold
the spindle.
She opens her hand to the poor, and reaches out her
hands to the needy.
She is not afraid of snow for her household, for all
her household are clothed in scarlet.
She makes herself coverings; her clothing is fine linen
and purple.
Her husband is known in the gates, when he sits among
the elders of the land.
She makes linen garments and sells them; she delivers
girdles to the merchant.
Strength and dignity are her clothing, and she laughs
at the time to come.
She opens her mouth with wisdom, and the teaching of
kindness is on her tongue.
She looks well to the ways of her household, and does
not eat the bread of idleness.
Her children rise up and call her blessed; her husband
also, and he praises her:
"Many women have done excellently, but you surpass them all."
Charm is deceitful, and beauty is vain, but a woman who
fears the Lord is to be praised.
Give her of the fruit of her hands, and let her works
praise her in the gates.

JUST GIRLS

The preceding theme program featured the boys as readers.
This next group of poems should be read by a choir of girls.
These poems are dainty and feminine and the arrangement of
voices should be varied, using solos, small groups and a full
chorus. Seat your chorus as informally as possible. Give the
girls nose-gays of flowers, flowers in their hair, pastel scarves
or gloves.

You will notice that the poet has helped you with your
interpretation by his arrangement of lines, lengths of lines,
and word placement. Do not be guided entirely by punctu-
ation and never forget the natural rhythm and cadence of the
literature.

CHANSONS INNOCENTES*

in Just—
spring   when the world is mud-
luscious the little
lame balloonman

whistles   far   and wee

and eddieandbill come
running from marbles and
piracies and it's
spring

when the world is puddle-wonderful

the queer
old balloonman whistles
far   and   wee
and bettyandisbel come dancing

from hop-scotch and jump-rope and

it's
spring
and
    the
        goat-footed
balloonman   whistles
far
and
wee

E.E. Cummings

DEAR MARCH

Dear March, come in!
How glad I am!
I looked for you before.
Put down your hat—
You must have walked—
How out of breath you are!
Dear March, how are you?
And the rest?
Did you leave Nature well?
Oh, March, come right upstairs with me
I have so much to tell!

I got your letter, and the bird's;
The maple never knew
That you were coming,—I declare,
How red their faces grew!
But, March, forgive me—
And all those hills
You left for me to hue;
There was no purple suitable,
You took it all with you.

Who knocks? That April!
Lock the door!
I will not be pursued!
He stayed away a year to call
When I am occupied.
But trifles look so trivial
As soon as you have come,
That blame is just as dear as praise
And praise as mere as blame.

Emily Dickinson

ONE PERFECT ROSE*

A single flow'r he sent me, since we met.
All tenderly his messenger he chose;
Deephearted, pure, with scented dew
        still wet—
One perfect rose.

I knew the language of the florist;
"My fragile leaves," it said, "his heart inclose"
Love long has taken for his amulet
One perfect rose.

Why is it no one ever sent me yet
One perfect limousine, do you suppose?
Oh no, it's always just my luck to get
One perfect rose.

                                        Dorothy Parker

*From *The Portable Dorothy Parker* Copyright 1926, ©renewed 1954 by Dorothy Parker. Reprinted by permission of The Viking Press.

ADVICE TO A GIRL*

No one worth possessing
Can be quite possessed;
Lay that on your heart,
My young angry dear:
This truth, this hard and precious stone,
Lay it on your hot cheek,
Let it hide your tear,
Hold it like a crystal
When you are alone
And gaze in the depths of the icy stone.

*Reprinted with permission of Macmillan Publishing Co., Inc., from *The Collected Poems of Sara Teasdale* (©1957). Copyright 1933 by Macmillian Publishing Co., Inc. Renewed 1961 by Guaranty Trust Company of New York, Executor.

Long, look long and you will be blessed
No one worth possessing
Can be quite possessed.

Sara Teasdale

A LADY THINKS SHE IS THIRTY*

Unwillingly Miranda wakes,
Feels the sun with terror,
One unwilling step she takes,
Shuddering to the mirror.

Miranda in Miranda's sight
Is old and gray and dirty;
Twenty-nine she was last night;
This morning she is thirty.

Shining like the morning star,
Like the twilight shining,
Haunted by a calendar,
Miranda sits a-pining.

Silly girl, silver girl,
Draw the mirror toward you;
Time who makes the year to whirl
Adorned as he adored you.

Time is timelessness for you;
Calendars for the human;
What's a year, or thirty, to
Loveliness made woman?

Oh, Night will not see thirty again,
Yet soft her wing, Miranda;
Pick up your glass and tell me, then—
How old is Spring, Miranda?

Ogden Nash

*From: *Verses from 1929 On*, by Ogden Nash, by permission of
Little, Brown and Co. ©1936 by Ogden Nash.

My Garden Gate

Build a garden trellis, free standing, and paint it white.
Dress the girls in white and give them each a sash, gloves, and
a basket of flowers to match her poem. Pose each in the gate
as she speaks and let her join the group arranged gracefully
around the gate. Use some appropriate background music.
The result is a charming nosegay of beauty.

MY GARDEN

Chorus   A garden is a lovesome thing, God wot!
Rose plot,
   Fringed pool,
Ferned grot—
The veriest school of peace;
and yet the fool contends
   That God is not—
Not God?
   in gardens?
      when the eve is cool?
Nay, but I have a sign;
'Tis very sure God walks in mine.

Thomas E. Brown

TO PRIMROSES FILLED WITH MORNING DEW*

Why do ye weep, sweet babes? Can tears
   Speak grief in you
   Who were but born
   Just as the modest morn
   Teemed her refreshing dew?
Alas, you have not known that shower

"My Garden" by Thomas E. Brown from *Choral Speaking
Arrangements for the Lower Grades.* by Louise Abney.
Reprinted by permission of Exposition Co. 1937

*From *The English Galaxy of Shorter Poems.* Buttrell, Gerald, ed. The
Macmillan Co. ©1934.

That mars a flower
Nor felt th' unkind
Breath of a blasting wind,
Nor are ye worn with years,
    Or warped, as we,
Who think it strange to see
Such pretty flowers, like to orphans young,
To speak by tears before ye have a tongue.

Speak, whimp'ring younglings, and make known
    The reason why
    Ye droop and weep.
    Is it for want of sleep,
    Or childish lullaby?
Or that ye have not seen as yet
    The violet,
    Or brought a kiss
From that sweet-heart to this?
No, no, this sorrow shown
    By your tears shed
Would have this lecture read,
That things of greatest, so of meanest worth,
Conceiv'd with grief are, and with tears brought forth.

Robert Herrick

TO VIOLETS*

Welcome, maids of honour,
    You do bring
    In the spring,
And wait upon her.

She has virgins many,
    Fresh and fair;
    Yet you are
More sweet than any.

*From the *English Galaxy of Shorter Poems.* Buttrell, Gerald, ed. The Macmillan Co. ©1934.

You're the maiden posies,
    And so graced
    To be placed
'Fore damask roses.

Yet though thus respected,
    By and by
    Ye do lie,
Poor girls, neglected.

                                    Robert Herrick

TO DAFFODILS*

Fair Daffodils, we weep to see
    You haste away so soon:
And yet the early-rising sun
    Has not attain'd his noon.
    Stay, stay
Until the hasting day
    Has run
    But to the even-song;
And, having pray'd together, we
    Will go with you along.

We have short time to stay, as you;
    We have as short a spring;
As quick a growth to meet decay,
    As you, or anything.
      We die
    As your hours do, and dry
      Away,
    Like to the summer's rain;
Or as the pearls of morning's dew,
    Ne'er to be found again.

                                    Robert Herrick

*From *The Oxford Book of Seventeenth Century Verse*, Grierson, H.J.C., and C. Bullough, ed. Reprinted by permission of Oxford University Press.©1934.

THE RHODORA*

In May, when sea-winds pierced our solitudes,
I found the fresh Rhodora in the woods,
Spreading its leafless blossoms in a damp nook,
To please the desert and the sluggish brook.
The purple petals, fallen in the pool,
Made the black water with their beauty gay;
Here might the redbird come his plumes to cool,
And court the flower that cheapens his array.
Rhodora! if the sages ask thee why
This charm is wasted on the earth and sky,
Tell them, dear, that if eyes were made for seeing,
Then Beauty is its own excuse for being:
Why thou wert there, O rival of the rose!
I never thought to ask, I never knew:
But, in my simple ignorance, suppose
The self-same Power that brought me there brought you.

Ralph Waldo Emerson

THE LILAC

Who thought of the lilac?
"I," dew said,
"I made up the lilac
out of my head."

"She made up the lilac!
Pooh!" thrilled a linnet,
and each dew-note had a
lilac in it.

Humbert Wolfe

*From *American Anthology 1787-1900*. Clarence Stedman, ed. Reprinted by permission Houghton, Mifflin Co.©1900.

A COMPARISON*

Apple blossoms look like snow,
They're different, though.
Snow falls softly, but it brings
Noisy things:
Sleighs and bells, forts and fights,
Cozy nights.
But apple blossoms when they go,
White and slow,
Quiet all the orchard space
Till the place
Hushed with falling sweetness seems
Filled with dreams.

John Farrar

QUEEN ANNE'S LACE

Queen Anne, Queen Anne, has washed her lace
    (She chose a summer day)
And hung it in a grassy place
    To whiten, if it may.

Queen Anne, Queen Anne, has left it there,
    And slept the dewy night;
Then waked, to find the sunshine fair,
    And all the meadows white.

Queen Anne, Queen Anne, is dead and gone
    (She died a summer's day),
But left her lace to whiten on
    Each weed-entangled way!

Mary Leslie Newton

*From *Bridled With Rainbows*, Burton, Sara and John E.
Burton, eds. Reprinted by permission Yale University Press.

WHITE AZALEAS*

Azaleas—whitest of white!
  White as the drifted snow
Fresh-fallen out of the night,
  Before the coming glow
Tinges the morning light;
  When the light is like the snow,
      white,
And the silence is like the light:
  Light, and silence, and snow,—
      All-white!

White! not a hint
Of the creamy tint
  A rose will hold,
  The whitest rose, in its inmost fold;
Not a possible blush;
White as an embodied hush;
  A VERY RAPTURE OF WHITE:
A wedlock of silence and light:
White, white as the wonder undefiled
Of Eve just wakened in Paradise;
Nay, white as the angel of a child
  That looks into God's own eyes!

                    Harriet McEwen Kimball

TO THE FRINGED GENTIAN*

Thou blossom bright with autumn dew,
And colored with the heaven's own blue,
That openest when the quiet light
Succeeds the keen and frosty night.

*From *American Anthology* 1787-1900. Clarence Stedman,
ed. Reprinted by permission, Houghton Mifflin Co. ©1900.

*From *American Anthology* 1787-1900. Clarence Stedman, ed.
Reprinted by permission, Houghton Mifflin Co. ©1900.

Thous comest not when violets lean
O'er wandering brooks and springs unseen,
Or columbines, in purple dressed,
Nod o'er the ground-bird's hidden nest.

Thou waitest late, and com'st alone
When woods are bare and birds are flown,
And frosts and shortening days portend
The aged year is near his end.

Then doth thy sweet and quiet eye
Look its fringes to the sky.
Blue—blue—as if that sky let fall
A flower from its cerulean wall.

I would that thus, when I shall see
The hour of death draw near to me,
Hope, blossoming within my heart,
May look to heaven as I depart.

William Cullen Bryant

THE GOLDEN ROD*

Spring is the morning of the year,
   And summer is the noontide bright;
The autumn is the evening clear,
   That comes before the winter's night.

And in the evening, everywhere
   Along the roadside, up and down,
I see the golden torches flare
   Like lighted street-lamps in the town.

I think the butterfly and bee,
   From distant meadows coming back,
Are quite contented when they see
   These lamps along the homeward track.

*From *Favorite Poems, Old and New*. Ferris, Helen Comp.
Reprinted by permission. Houghton Mifflin Company ©1957.

But those who stay too late get lost;
   For when the darkness falls about,
Down every lighted street the Frost
   Will go and put the torches out!

Frank Dempster Sherman

ROSEMARY*

Beauty and Beauty's son and rosemary—
Venus and Love, her son, to speak plainly—
born of the sea supposedly,
at Christmas each, in company,
braids a garland of festivity.
   Not always rosemary,—
since the flight to Egypt blooming differently.
With lancelike leaf, green but silver underneath,
its flowers—white originally—
turned blue. The herb of memory,
imitating the blue robe of Mary
   is not too legendary
to snare symbolism in its pungency.
Springing from stones beside the sea,
the height of Christ when thirty-three—
no higher—it feeds on dew and to the bee
"hath a dumb language"; is in reality
   a kind of Christmas tree.

Marianne Moore

Chorus: The kiss of the sun for pardon
      the song of the birds for mirth
One is nearer God's heart in a garden
   Than anywhere else on earth.

Dorothy Blomfield

*Copyright ©1954 by Conde Nast Publications, Inc.

T.S. Eliot's "Cats."

The famous author of *Murder in the Cathedral* has given to us also some delightful poems about cats. If you like cats and understand them, you will appreciate the poems and perhaps recognize your own favorite cat. They are naturals for exciting rhythm. Display this rhythm with voice, muscle tone, facial expression and total bodily involvement. Use two dancers with "The Song of the Jellicles." Dress one in white leotards and one in black leotards, with matching half masks.

THE RUM TUM TUGGER*

Chorus	The Rum Tum Tugger is a Curious Cat:
	If you offer him pheasant he would rather have grouse.
5 boys	If you put him in a house he would much perfer a flat.
do this	
as a	If you put him in a flat then he'd rather have a house.
round	If you set him on a mouse then he only wants a rat.
	If you set him on a rat then he'd rather chase a mouse.
Chorus	Yes the Rum Tum Tugger is a Curious Cat—
	And there isn't any call for me to shout it:
	for he will do oo oo
	as he do oo oo
	and there's no doing anything about it!
Chorus	The Rum Tum Tugger is a terrible bore:
	When you let him in, then he wants to be out;
	He's always on the wrong side of every door,
round	And as soon as he's at home, then he'd like to get about.
	He likes to lie in the bureau drawer,
	but he makes such a fuss if he can't get out.
Chorus	Yes the Rum Tum Tugger is a Curious Cat—
	And it isn't any use for you to doubt it
	for he will do oo oo
	as he do do oo oo
	and there's no doing anything about it!

Chorus	The Rum Tum Tugger is a curious beast;
	His disobliging ways are a matter of habit.
	If you offer him fish then he always wants a feast;
	when there isn't any fish then he won't eat rabbit.
round	If you offer him cream then he sniffs and sneers,
	for he only likes what he finds for himself;
	so you'll catch him in it right up to the ears,
	if you put it away on the larder shelf.
Chorus	The Rum Tum Tugger is artful and knowing,
	The Rum Tum Tugger doesn't care for a cuddle;
	but he'll leap on your lap in the middle of your sewing,
	for there's nothing he enjoys like a horrible muddle.
	Yes the Rum Tum Tugger is a Curious Cat—
	And there isn't any need for me to spout it;
	for he will do oo
	as he do do oo
	and there's no doing anything about it!

THE NAMING OF CATS*

Chorus	The Naming of Cats is a difficult matter/
	It isn't just one of your holiday games/
Soloists	You may think at first I'm as mad as a hatter
should	
stand	When I tell you, a cat must have THREE DIFFERENT
then sit	NAMES/
	First of all, there's the name that the family use daily/

solo 1   solo 2   solo 3   solo 4
Such as Peter, Augustus, Alonzo, or James—/

*From *Old Possum's Book of Practical Cats.* Copyright 1939 by T.S. Eliot; copyrighted 1967 by Erma Valeria Eliot. Reprinted by permission of Harcourt Brace Jovanovich, Inc.

                solo 5   solo 6   solo 7   solo 8
Such as Victor, or Jonathan, George, or Bill Bailey—/
  All of them sensible everyday names.
There are fancier names if you think they sound sweeter
                    women   men
Some for the gentlemen/ some for the dames:/
solo 9   solo 10   solo 11   solo 12
Such as Plato, Admetus, Electra, Demeter—/
  But all of them sensible everyday names./
But I tell you, a cat needs a name that's particular,/
  A name that's peculiar, and more dignified,
Else how can he keep up his tail perpendicular,
  Or spread out his whiskers, or cherish his pride?/
Of names of this kind, I can give you a quorum,/
          Solo 1   solo 2   solo 3
Such as Munkustrap, Quaxo, or Coricopat,/

          Solo 4   Solo 5
Such as Bombalarina, or else Jellylorum—/
  Names that never belong to more than one cat./
But above and beyond there's still one name left over,/
  And that is the name that you will never will guess./
The name that no human research can discover—/
  But the CAT HIMSELF KNOWS, and will never
      confess/
When you notice a cat in profound meditation,/
  The reason, I tell you is always the same;
His mind is engaged in a rapt comtemplation
  Of the thought,/ of the thought,/ of the thought of
          his name;/
          His ineffable effable/
          Effanineffable/
Deep and inscrutable singular Name./

THE SONG OF THE JELLICLES*

Chorus
with
dancers

Jellicle Cats come out tonight

Jellicle Cats come one come all:
The Jellicle Moon is shining bright—
Jellicles come to the Jellicle Ball

Jellicle Cats are black and white,
Jellicle Cats are rather small;
Jellicle Cats are merry and bright,
And pleasant to hear when they caterwaul.
Jellicle Cats have cheerful faces,
Jellicle Cats have bright black eyes;
They like to practice their airs and graces
And wait for the Jellicle Moon to rise.

Jellicle Cats develop slowly,
Jellicle Cats are not too big;
Jellicle Cats are roly-poly,
They know how to dance a gavotte and a jig.
Until the Jellicle Moon appears
They make their toilette and take their repose:
Jellicles wash behind their ears,
Jellicles dry between their toes.

Jellicle Cats are white and black,
Jellicle Cats are of moderate size;
Jellicles jump like a jumping-jack,
Jellicle Cats have moonlit eyes.
They're quiet enough in the morning hours,
They're quiet enough in the afternoon,
Reserving their terpsichorean powers
To dance by the light of the Jellicle Moon.

Solo	Jellicle Cats are black and white, Jellicle Cats (as I said) are small; If it happens to be a stormy night They will practice a caper or two in the hall. If it happens the sun is shining bright You would say they had nothing to do at all: They were resting and saving themselves to be right For the Jellicle Moon and the Jellicle Ball
	(Observe the rhythm of the dancers and read to accompany them).

You may wish to include other selections from this same collection by T.S. Eliot.

Is This Violence?

Rev. Nulton's original essay, "America the Beautiful," may be used as an introduction for a theme program depicting contemporary problems. Search through magazines and recent literature for ideas. Some ideas are:

> "Hoodlums" by Carl Sandburg
> "The Laughers" by Louis Untermeyer
> "The Last Flower" by James Thurber

AMERICA THE BEAUTIFUL

Chorus hums before readers begin Stop humming here	Oh beautiful for spacious skies, for amber. . .yes—America the Beautiful— This is our land—The land of freedom, wealth and beauty. All is beautiful we say—all is well—but all is not so good, all is not so well. Somewhere deep in the heart of our cities is a child reaching into a garbage can for his evening meal. No—all is not so good—all is not so well.

Some place in the mass cracker boxes
called homes in Suburbia—is a teenager lost
from the necessity of love and home by a
father or mother who has left a once happy
home because of some senseless quarrel.
No—all is not so good—all is not so well.
Deep in the ghettos a Negro cries
"Police Brutality" and the flames of burning
buildings and rock-shattered windows explode
across the T.V. screen and "White Backlash"
builds up its intolerance to human suffering.
No—all is not so good. . .All is not so well.
In the midst of a college classroom, a
theologian claims "God is Dead" and whatever
faith the student has is shattered by a
seemingly religious man who has yet to discover
the wonder of salvation! No—all is not so
good. . . .All is not so well.

Paul Nulton
Northwestern College
Choral Reader

CITIES

Use some or all of these poems to carry out a "city"
theme. A student who lives in Chicago took pictures of these
familiar city scenes and we projected them on a gauze curtain
or screen behind the readers during the reading of "Skyscraper."

SKYSCRAPER*

Chorus
By day the skyscraper looms in the smoke and the sun has
a soul./ Prairie and valley,/ streets of the city,/ pour people
into it and they mingle among its twenty floors and are
poured out again and back to the streets,/ prairies/ and
valleys./

*From *Complete Poems of Carl Sandburg*, copyright 1950 by Carl
Sandburg. Reprinted by permission of Harcourt Brace Jovanovich, Inc.

It is the men and women, boys and girls so poured in and out all day that give the building a soul/ of dreams and thoughts and memories./ (Dumped in the sea or fixed in a desert,/ who would care for the building or speak its name or ask a policeman the way to it?)/ Elevators slide on their cables and tubes catch letters and parcels/ and iron pipes carry gas and water in and sewage out./ Wires climb with secrets, carry light and carry words, and tell terrors and profits and loves—/ curses of men grappling plans of business/ and questions of women in plots of love./ Hour by hour the caissons reach down to the rock of the earth and hold the building to a turning planet./ Hour by hour the girders play as ribs/ and reach out and hold together the stone walls and floors./ Hour by hour the hand of the mason and the stuff of the mortar clinch the pieces and parts to the shape an architect voted./ Hour by hour the sun and the rain,/ the air and the rust,/ and the press of time running into centuries,/ play on the building inside and out and use it./ Men who sunk the pilings and mixed mortar are laid in graves/ where the wind whistles a wild song without words./ And so are men who strung the wires and fixed the pipes and tubes and those who saw it rise floor by floor./ Souls of them all are here,/ even the hod carrier begging at back doors hundreds of miles away/ and the bricklayer who went to state's prison for shooting another man while drunk./ (One man fell from a girder and broke his neck at the end of a straight plunge—/ he is hero—/ his soul gone into the stones of the building)./

On the office doors from tier to tier/—hundreds of names/ and each name standing for a face written across/ with a dead child,/ a passionate lover,/ a driving ambition for a million dollar business/ or a lobster's ease of life. Behind the signs on the doors they work/ and the walls tell nothing from room to room./

Ten-dollar-a-week stenographers take letters from corporation officers,/lawyers,/ efficiency engineers/and tons of letters go bundled from the building to all ends of the earth./ Smiles and tears of each office girl go into the soul of the building just the same as the master-men who rule the building. Hands of clocks turn to noon hours and each floor empties its men and women who go away and eat and come back to work./ Toward the end of the afternoon all work slackens and all jobs go slower as the people feel day closing on them./

Slowly one by one the floors are emptied./. . .The uniformed elevator men are gone./ Pails clang./. . .Scrubbers work talking in foreign tongues. Broom and water and mops clean from the floors human dust and spit,/and machine grime of the day. Spelled in electric fire on the roof are words telling miles of houses and people where to buy a thing for money. The sign speaks till midnight./ Darkness on the hallways./ Voices echo./ Silence holds./ Watchmen walk slow from floor to floor and try the doors./ Revolvers bulge from their hip pockets./ Steel safes stand in corners./ Money is stacked in them./

Solo

A young watchman leans at a window and sees the lights of barges butting their way across a harbor, nets of red and white lanterns in a railroad yard, and a span of gloom splashed with lines of white and blurs or crosses and clusters over the sleeping city.

Chorus

By night the skyscraper looms in the smoke and the stars and has a soul/.

Carl Sandburg

A CITY IS. . .*

Solo	A city is tall buildings
Chorus	What else is a city—
Solo	A city is pizza places
Chorus	What else is a city—
Solo	A city is restaurants
Chorus	What else is a city—
Solo	A city is libraries

*Reprinted by permission of The Public Library of the City of Boston.

Chorus	What else is a city—
Solo	A city is marzipans
Chorus	What else is a city—
Solos,	A city is cars, trucks, buses
each reader	
picks up cue	A city is the ocean
quickly al-	
ternating.	A city is a sky
	A city is a feast
	A city is houses
	A city is cemeteries
	A city is swimming pools
	A city is trees
	A city is apartment houses
	A city is an elevated train
	A city is subways
	A city is stores
	A city is bridges
	A city is flags
	A city is noise
	A city is ships
	A city is airplanes
	A city is helicopters
	A city is clouds
	A city is a parade
	A city is schools
	A city is the YMCA
	A city is Paul Revere's Mall
	A city is the Public Garden
	A city is Paul Revere's house
Chorus	*A city is a city!!!*

by Diane Farrell and
Ruth M. Hayes

MAMIE

Solo

Mamie beat her head against the bars of the little Indiana town and dreamed of romance and big things off somewhere the way the railroad trains all ran. She could see the smoke of the engines get lost down where the streaks of steel flashed in the sun and when the newspapers came in on the morning mail, she knew there was a big Chicago far off, where all the trains ran.

She got tired of the barber shop boys and the post office chatter and the church gossip and the old pieces the band played on the Fourth of July and Decoration Day.

And sobbed at her fate and beat her head against the bars and was going to kill herself. When the thought came to her that if she was going to die she might as well die struggling for a clutch of romance among the streets of Chicago.

She has a job at six dollars a week in the basement of the Boston Store. And even now she beats her head against the bars in the same old way and wonders if there is a bigger place the railroads run to Chicago where maybe there is romance
and big things
and real dreams
that never go smash.

Carl Sandburg

THREE PIECES ON NIGHT OVER THE CITY

I

(one dancer)

Solo
girl

Think of being eye level with a star!

A lustrous, great white star in the blue
infinity of sky over the city!

And I walked the street below holding
my hat against the gusty wind around
the corner guildings, plodding the
day's last journey home.
Then out of high windows a star—
eye-level with me!

II

(two dancers)

Solo
girl

Oh blue sky and night—deep, night—

blue sky and bright, white moon!
And the city—with a million odd
Points and angles, jagged silhouettes
against the blue, queer dunce-capped
heads on solid squared shoulders.
The city lays each pointed head,
nestles each squared shoulder into
the deep down of night and sleeps;
while I hold vigil alone from my
high window, late and alone, and feel
a prayer go out of me.
Oh blue sky and night—
deep, night-blue sky and bright, white moon!

III

(three dancers)

Chorus
softly
dreamily

"Euclid alone has looked on Beauty bare."

The city is limned against the sky
tonight./
Scintillating lines of light in planes
of black under a moon-flooded arc,/
spherical dome of midnight blue/
lines,/ planes/ spheres.—/
Beauty bare against the sky tonight!/

(The readers will follow the dancer's interpretation of the poem)

Helen Gertrude Hicha

99

NIGHT COMES TO THE CITY

Women	'Round upon our little globe,
	the gracious gloaming goes,
Read	Touching his fingers
Smoothly	to the cheek of each
and	hemisphere/
Meaning-	The vagabond dealer in
fully	shadows *flings* out his dusks
	to the city,/

And *hurls* the hot sun below the
horizon,/
Pursuing the light down the long
city buildings
'Till the wake of the sunset must
show
A thousand Rasputins unbinding their
lucent gold hair./
The Mutual Trust building has
windows as bright as new pennies/
Dazzling the eyes of the weary
shoppers,
Who look with relief at the six
o'clock sky/
Lands of purple and pink wane in
the west/
Land above the North Station, the
evening star
Quickens and burns. . . ./

Men	Down the full streets come the six o'clock buses,	
	Swelled to the seams with commuters:/	
Solo	Let me off at Fifth street, please—	*(girls with*
Solo	Driver, take my fare—	*various hats)*
Solo	I want a round trip ticket—	
Solo	Mister, please don't push!	
Men	Okay everybody, the back end's going the same place	
(Conductor)	as the front end, so step lively and step to the rear!	

Women	The peanut man lights the blue flame in his vendor:
Men	Peanuts! Get um hot! Peanuts!
Women	The newboys call the late edition:
Men	Evening final! Get your e-e-evening f-i-i-nal!
Women	And row by row, the street lamps flicker on./ These are the last few moments For children in the darkening streets/
Solo	I have a little doggie and he won't bite you And he won't bite you! But he will bite you!
3 Women *(sing)*	All around the mulberry bush The monkey chased the weasel That's the way the money goes, Pop! Goes the weasel!
Solo	Allee allee all infree! Allee Allee all infree!
Women	The mothers lean from the windows And call to the children:
Solo	Donald!
Solo	Ronald
Solo	Harry!
Solo	Mary!
Solo	Larry!
Solo	A-a-a-algernon!
Men	H-e-e-ey Butch! (with hat) Allee allee all in free,
Solo	Allee allee all in free, Allee allee all in free,
Chorus	Now the impartial dark has completely come/ Innumerable stars glisten and gleam/ Below them the marquees wink out the night's entertainment/ The pleasure crowd gathers/

(girls with
curler caps, etc.)

101

Woman	Oh, ha ha!/ oh, how gay!/
	I don't believe a word you say/
	Clever words don't take me in—/
	But say those charming things
	again!/
Men	Oh, ha ha! come on, smile!
Solo Men	Here are two seats along the
	aisle.
Solo Men	Here's an orchid— *(with props)*
Solo Men	Here's a sable—
Solo Men	Here's a waiter and a ringside table.
Woman	Oh, ha ha!/ La Vie, La Vie!/
	Tres chic/ tres cher/ tres gai are we!/
Women	Outside the garish cafes
	A slip of a new moon arises, clean-
	silver and free/
	And somewhere on a lonely beat
	A lonely policeman whistles for
	luck to his moon./
	New Moons for new loves—/
Chorus	Two by two the couples steal from
	the streets,
	Swinging hands,/they come to the
	park
	Where an indistinct breeze sifts
	through the tousled trees./
	They hold trysts by the pond
	where the water laps soft in
	the fountain,/
	And they whisper/and whisper/ and
	whisper/ into the hush of the night./
Solo	If I should speak
Men	All my heart has prompted
	Would you stay
	Would you listen
	Would you care?
Solo	If you should speak
Women	Oh, how I would listen!
	Anytime
	Any place
	Anywhere—

Chorus	This is a love that night has wrought From silver and silence and bliss./ What night has revealed,/must always be sealed—/ With a look—/ With a smile—/ With a kiss./ The lovers go home, swinging hands And one by one, the lights blink out Until the city lies in gentle shadow./ The drowsy souls of the citizens Slip one by one into the silent sea of sleep./ *(men "bong"*
Women *Couples* *move out,* *suiting* *the* *action to* *the* *words*	Midnight—/ *the hours)* The buildings of the city stand like dumb dark giants Under a wash of moonlight./ Flocks of stars begin their noise- less circuit/ Midnight—/ The bridges rear like filigree over the ebony rivers Leading out of the city and down to the seas/ Midnight/ The clocks boom the hour to unlistening ears/ Bidding the city a very good night-/ A very good night-/ A very good night—!/

Place girls on one side, boys on
the other, with an aisle in between.
Members of the group should drama-
tize the words.

Claire Boiko

103

GO TELL IT IN THE CITY

Man	So I came to the city because I wanted to get ahead
Solo	"He that exalteth himself shall be humbled."
Chorus	Get ahead. . ./.make money./. .buy a car, a bigger car./. .make money/ . .money./. .get ahead!/
Man	But I can't find a place to live. We haven't much money. I can't pay the rent they ask. I can't find a place. . .I can't find a place.
Chorus	I want a *big* car/ I want a *big* house/
Chorus	I want a *big* job.
Solo	"A man's life consisteth not in the abundance of the things which he possesseth."
Man	But I want to get ahead. . .if I can find a place to live. . . .
Chorus	Crowded housing/. .crowds/. .noise./. three families in one room/. .forty thousand in a trailer camp./. .no room/. .no room./.crowds/. . . the CITY./
Man	My children have no place to play. . .we can't pay the rent in a better street. . .it's so noisy here. . .but I want to get ahead.
Chorus	Noise/. .noise/. .crowds/. .no place to play/. .no place to rest./. .children playing on pavements/. . babies sleeping on pavements/. .no room/. .no room/. . get ahead/. .the City./
Solo	"What shall it profit a man if he gain the whole world and lose his own soul?"
Man	I've looked up and down the streets for a familiar face. . .you can be awfully lonesome in a crowd. . . and the subways roaring. . .and the old people. . .and the children. . .I'm afraid here!
Chorus	Roar of subways/. .roar of machines/. .crowd. . .crime/. . noise/. .alone/.,.get ahead/. .the CITY./
Solo	"Go tell it in the city that Jesus Christ is Lord."
Chorus	Yes! Go tell it in the city,/tell it in city/. . . . Jesus Christ is Lord!/

(The male soloist moves about restlessly as he speaks.)

Life Magazine, October 31, 1969, is devoted to poems, essays and photographs of cities. The essay "The City Zooms In" could be used effectively with projections.

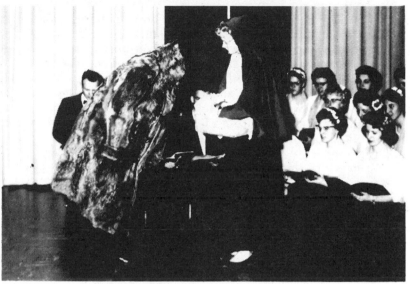

The Little Girl and the Wolf.

Feature Numbers for School or Club

THE LITTLE GIRL AND THE WOLF*

Men   One afternoon a big wolf waited in a dark forest for a little girl to come along carrying a basket of food to her grandmother.

Women   Finally a little girl did come along and she was carrying a basket of food.

(high
voices)   (Men whistle)

Men   "Are you carrying that basket to your grandmother?" asked the wolf.

Women	The little girl said yes, she was.
Men	So the wolf asked her where her grandmother lived, and the little girl told him/ and he disappeared into the woods. Ha ha (he disappears with wolf laugh).
Chorus	When the little girl opened the door of her grandmother's house/she saw that there was somebody in bed with a nightcap and nightgown on./ She had approached no nearer than twenty-five feet from the bed/ when she saw that is was not her grandmother,/ but the wolf!/ For even in a nightcap,/ a wolf does not look any more like your grandmother than the Metro-Goldwyn lion looks like Calvin Coolidge./ So the little girl took an automatic out of her basket—and shot the wolf dead. (bang, bang, bang)
Three small girls high voices	The moral to this story is: It is not so easy to fool little girls nowadays—as it used to be!

James Thurber

This is an old favorite and its use will add a bit of fun to your program. Use a red cap and basket for the little girl and an old raccoon coat over the head of the wolf (here characters should pantomime the action). You might cut a two dimensional bedstead from cardboard or wood, paint it to represent the bed and leave a place for "grandma" to stick out her head, covered with a nightcap.

DON'T ASK ME, I JUST LIVE HERE*

Chorus	Americans once got up asking themselves only about the weather. Today we awake to ask who we are and what it all means. A noted humorist, as confused as the rest of us, issues his comment on our times—
Solo	"Two plasticburgers, a slice of mucilage and a glass of carbon dioxide, and make it fast, honey, I've only got 20 minutes to catch my coronary."

* ©1969 by Russell Baker. Reprinted by permission of Harold Matson Co., Inc. First printed in *Life Magazine*.

Group I	"Pst! The computers took over at midnight. Pass it on." (chant as a computer—no rhythm)
Group II	"The computers took over at midnight. Pass it on."
Group III	"The computers took over at midnight. Pass it on."
Chorus	"The computers took over at midnight. Pass it on."
Chorus	We over-30's are the ones who really made the revolution. What we did was create a whole new stage of man. It used to be that you had adolescence and then you finished school and went to work and became an adult. We inserted another stage—youth—by ordering everybody off to college at the end of adolescence. This gave us a whole new class highly educated people who could afford the luxury of applying adult critical faculties to our society because they weren't going to lose jobs or adult sensibilities, they were uniquely equipped not only to criticize our flaws but also to act. They're not usually very tolerant of those who dress differently from them, and that could be bad.
	A hundred years ago Walt Whitman heard America singing. Lucky man. Nowadays he'd see America spectating. There's so much spectating going on that a lot of us never get around to listening. Life is always walking up to us and saying. (Solo) "Come on in, the living's fine,
Chorus	"and what do we do? Back off and take its picture. Freeze it dead in a little box. Or have somebody else box it for us so we can stare at it in the dark. With sunglasses we wear our dark in the sunlight. They make us faceless, a good thing to be if you want to discourage life from winking at you and saying, (Solo) "There's a hell of a good time out here, let's go." (Chorus) A few go. They're the ones who still hear America singing.
	The nudity crowd tells you, (Solo) "The

human body is beautiful." (Chorus) Don't they
know that tigers and horses and weasels have
been laughing at it for eons? Except for a few
oddities, like Tarzan and Raquel Welch, the
human body is one of the ugliest bodies around.
This is because it isn't covered with hair, scales,
hide or feathers. (Solo 1) Did you ever see a
snake with a potbelly, (Solo 2) An antelope

Chorus   with varicose veins? (Solo 3) A bluebird with
freckles? You probably would if they took off
their covering and pranced around naked.

Solo 1   How should one American introduce himself
to another nowadays? Do you say, (Solo 2) "Hi,
there, I'm your friendly guilty white oppressor,
and I don't want you to feel bad about hating
me because I deserve to be hated, and if you
only know how guilty I feel. . . . Too many of us
come on like this. Guilt is the emotional fashion.
It's chic, like sideburns and miniskirts, and it's
dangerous, and it doesn't get us anywhere, and
for all these reasons it's comtemptible at this
moment in history. But how do you begin if you
bog down right at the start quarreling about
what words you're supposed to think in? Do
you say (Group I) "Negroes," (Group II)
"Blacks," (Group III Chorus) "Afros"? Should I
resent being called white (actually I'm pink in
summer and gray in winter)? I didn't know any
"Blacks" or "Grays" or "Afros" or "Pinks."
(Solo 1) I know a few people. They are all kinds
of people. I'd like to start there.

"My fellow Americans, I am sure that you
will agree with me when I assert—here tonight—
my firm belief that there is no place in America
today for those who have lost faith in the power
and the dignity and the glory of the individual."

Where are we going? That's easy. We're sailing
right into the history books, which is about the
dullest place you can end up. The important
question is, do you make the trip as gracefully as
you can with what you've got?

Chorus   Hello. . . . . . .PE 6-5300?. . . . .
                    When is grown-up?
                    Why is honor?
                    Who is America?
                    Where is God?
                    Which I is me?
                    What is—?

Russell Baker
Life July 25, 1969

Don't Ask Me, I Just Live Here, by Russell Baker, is adapted from an article in *Life* magazine, July 25, 1969. Projections can be used at strategic points. The current magazines will supply you with many ideas. Make transparencies using the illustrations and use an overhead projector.

THE REAL THING

by Jeff Zwagerman

(Note: The commercial jingles can be sung in tune or changed to speaking at the preference of the director)

The scene opens with the group entering the placement area with Kazoo's playing Yankee Doodle. Group members can be in any order but the narrator should be in back on a step ladder.

Narrator: All right America, about two centuries ago something fabulous happened right here, to us. Tell us the significance of that date in U.S. History. America, what is important about 1776?

(All look at each other and mumble)

109

All: 200 years ago we had our first Bi-Centennial
          minute?

Narrator: Wrong America. Try again.

All: Ronald McDonald invented the Big Mac?

Narrator: Get serious, America.

All: Ewell Gibbons got heartburn from posion Ivy
          and invented the Grape Nut.

Narrator: One more chance America.

All: George Washington took his first Bayer Break
          at Valley Forge.

Narrator: What is it with you people?

All: (All hum America through the next speech until the
          Narrator says "Think about it."

Narrator: In 1776 our United States became a nation. Men
          put down their lives for their country. History
          has progressed. The Declaration of Indepen-
          dence was signed. We ratified the constitution.
          Great Presidents have come and gone. Two
          world wars have been fought. Millions and
          millions of people have been born and died. We
          have celebrated our first Bi-Centennial. Just
          think about all that happened in a few hundred
          years. Think about it! All right now, what does
          America really mean to us?

All: Baseball.

Narrator: (Echoes)   Baseball.

All: Hot Dogs.

Narrator: Hot Dogs.

All: Apple Pie

Narrator: Apple Pie.

All: And Chevrolet.

Narrator: (Reacts as if going to say it, then does a double take and looks puzzled.) Chevrolet? What do you mean; Chevrolet?

All: (Singing) We love baseball, hot dogs, apple pie and chevrolet. Baseball, hot dogs, apple pie and chevrolet. Baseball, hot dogs, apple pie and. . .

Solo 1:   (Cuts groups off) In my merry Oldsmobile, in my merry Oldsmobile.

Narrator: (Interrupts) Hold it, hold it, I don't understand all this. Now what is it you really love, America?

All: (Spoken) We love Baseball, Hot dogs, Apple Pie. . . . and Chevrolet.

Narrator: But what does Chevrolet got to do with the American spirit?

All: What has Chevrolet got to do with the American Spirit?

Solo 1:   Hey, tell em Alvin.

Alvin: (Very goofy type) Da——I don't know.

All: Aw Alvin.

Solo 2:   Hit it gang. (Group hums Glory, Glory Hallelujah) As a typical American to the Republic for which our group stands, one nation, indivisible, with liberty and justice for. . . . the commerical!

         (Group changes humming to "Nobody Knows the Trouble I've Seen.")

Yes friends, all our lives we're bombarded with ads by magazines and newspapers, radio and television, billboards and brochures.

Solo 3: What could be more American than the advertisment? What's more, television commericals are better entertainment than the actual programs, indeed they are the one remaining hope for our vast wasteland. What could be more entertaining than. . .

All: Watching a German Shepherd go for Mr. Wipple's throat as he takes his last squeeze of the Charmin.

Solo 4: Hi, I'd like to talk to you about. . . .diarrhea. So the next time you get diarrhea you'll thank me. . . . .for the Pepto Bismol.

All: After Mrs. Olson has worked hard on preparing her masterpiece pot of Butternut Coffee, old Herb walks in and takes a sip, slowly puts the cup down, and begins to walk out. His wife asks. . . .

Solo
Wife: Where are you going honey?

Solo
Herb: Back to cleaning the septic tank. That's the third cup you've made me this morning and it still taste terrible.

Solo 5: You see? Now what could be more interesting than that?

Solo 6: (Group should hum the Star Spangled Banner through the next two Solos) Did you know the first radio program occurred on August 28, 1922 when WNBC Broadcasted a ten minute talk sponsored by the Queensboro Long Island Realty Company?

Solo 7:   In 1948 the Milton Berle Show is credited with doing more to stimulate television set buying than any other factor. But that's a misconception. For without advertisement there wouldn't have been any Milton Berle and radio and television would have gone broke years ago.

Solo 2:   So what's more American than.....

Girls: (Sung) My seamless isn't shapeless anymore.

Solo 2:   Or how would you know that......

All: (Sung) You can trust your car to the man who wears the star, the big bright Texaco Star.

Solo 9:   Hey, have you got something for a headache?

All: Hey, Have we got something for a headache. (Group makes sign of victory and sings:) Ta Ta Ta Da.

Guys: To look sharp and to feel sharp too get the razor that's made right for you. Light, regular heavy beard too. It's the finest shave that you can get. . . .Gilette.

Solo 10: LSMFT—Lucky Strike means fine tobacco.

All: Winston tastes good like a (Bump, Bump) cigarette should.

Solo 11: Hey, that's bad grammar.

All: Not bad grammar just good taste.

Solo 12: (Old Home Commerical spoken like C.W. Mc-Call) I was truckin' real hard just north of Cleaver and feelin' kinda low cuz I just hit a beaver. Yah sort of splattered him all over the road. The blood, the fur, and the innards.

All: Pretty Yecky.

Solo 12:   Well I needed a break cuz Sloan licked my ear so
            I let him outside and he cleaned my tire and I
            walked on in to the Keep on Truckin' Cafe.

All: Grease city.

Solo 12:   Well, Mavis was there and she threw me a roll, I
            chewed it up and swallowed real slow, cuz it was
            dry and tasted like fried crow. I needed a cup of
            hot "C". The coffee's so hot I fell off the stool.
            Picked myself up and felt like a fool, so I kissed
            Mavis real good til she started to drool.

All: Wet sneakers.

Solo 12:   I slipped into the truck and I feel kinda cruel
            cuz I haven't been back not even for fuel at the
            Old Home filler up and Keep on Truckin' Cafe.

All: At Pis——gah. Love it or leave it.

All: (Sung) You deserve a break today, so get up and
            get on your way to. . .(chanted) all beef patties
            special sauce, lettuce, cheese, pickles, onions on
            a sesame seed bun.

Solo 2:   Commercials America—That's truly what makes
            our country tick. We know more about our-
            selves and others know more about us through
            what we buy.

Solo 2
con.:   And what do we buy? Well things like: *Chewing Gum*

Girls: (Sing) Double your pleasure, double your fun,
            with double good, double rich, doublemint gum.

All: Get that just brushed freshness with Dentyne.

Guys: (Sung) Wriggles Spearmint gum, gum, gum. . . .

114

Girls:	(Sung at the same time as above) Let's pick a pack of Juicy Fruit gum. Let's pick a pack from the juicy fruit tree.
Solo 2:	*UNDERWEAR*
Cosell Voice:	Hello, this is Howard Cosell on top of Mt. Everest for fruit of the loom underwear saying— it's pretty cold up here without my pants on.
Solo 14:	I've just discovered this exciting new bra, that I've just got to show it to somebody.
Guys:	(Wolf whistle)
All:	Hanes makes you feel good all under.
Solo 15:	Cross your heart
Solo 16:	I can't believe it's a girdle, girdle.
Solo 12:	*DEODORANT*
Solo 17:	I haven't used my deodorant today and I probably won't use it tomorrow either.
All:	We know—We know.
Solo 18:	My coat told me I need new right guard. Whew!
All:	Use Arrid to be sure.
Solo 2:	*TOOTHPASTE*
All:	Crest has been shown to be an effective, decay preventing dentifrice when used in a con- scientiously applied program of oral hygiene and regular professional care.
Solo 17:	Look ma, no cavities.

Solo 20: Jimmy, put your dentures back in your mouth.

Girls: (Sexy) Ultra Bright gives your mouth,
sex appeal. (Blow Kiss)

Solo 2: *DETERGENT*

Solo 21: (Chanted) He's got ring around the collar,
ring around the collar.

All: (Chanted) Tide clean keeps on working after
other suds have quit.

Solo 22: Can I rip up your shirt to prove a point?

All: Oxydol, with bleach that cleans.

Solo 2: *BREATH FRESHENERS*

Solo 23: The old man's too much for ya huh?

Solo 24: It's your breath dad. It stinks.

All: Certs is two—two—two mints in one.

Solo 25: Wanna really shake up your mouth?

All: Listerine, the taste you hate twice a day.

Solo 2: You know, for almost any brand in existence
there is some type of advertising. Some day
while you're walking down the street, yell out
some brand names and see what happens.
Like. . . . . .FORD.

All: (Sing) We're having a wall to wall clearance sale.
We're gonna get rid of them all. So if you've
waiting now the time is right, cuz the Fords are
wall to wall.

Solo 2:   *BURGER KING*

All: Have it your way—have it your way. Hold the
            pickles, hold the lettuce, special orders don't
            upset us, all we ask is that you let us serve it
            your way. (Should be sung)

Solo 2:   *OSCAR MEYER*

Solo 26:   I wish I were an Oscar Meyer Wiener.

Solo 2:   *AMERICAN EXPRESS*

All: It's dangerous to carry cash.

Solo 2:   *Bounty*

All: The quicker picker upper.

Solo 2:   *SERTA*

Girls: Buy a perfect sleeper—buy a perfect sleeper
            —perfect sleeper—buy Serta.

Solo 2:   *BAND AID*

Solo 27:   (Sung) I am stuck on band aid cuz band aid's
            stuck on me.

Solo 2:   *Hardy's*

All: Well hello Hardies, hello Hardies
            It's so nice to have you back where you belong.

Solo 28:   Did you ever think of how effective commericals
            really are? How many of the old ones do you
            remember? Could you still supply the brand?
            How about?

Solo:

1: What has a better idea?
2: From the land of sky blue water
3: Hottest brand going
4: Only you can prevent forest fires
5: 99 & 44 100% pure—it floats
6: You'll wonder where the yellow went when you brush your teeth with. . . . . .
7: "Good to the very last drop"
8: "From the valley of the jolly. . .Ho. .Ho. .Ho"
9: "I'd walk a mile for a. . . ."
10: What comes from contented cows?
11: How are quaker puffed cereals made?
12: Theres always room for. . . .
13: Which soft drink "hits the spot"?
14: Soft Strong and pops up too
15: He's feeling his. . . .
16: Breakfast of champions
17: A little dab will do ya.
18: Wherever particular people congregate they smoke. . . .
19: "Call for Phillip Morris"
20: When if rains it pours.
21: The batteries with nine lives.
22: The candy mint with the hole.
23: Known for its 57 varieties
24: Mountain grown
25: These are uncola nuts actually
26: You only go around once in life, so grab for all the gusto you can.

Solo 2: You see America? Commercials are important. They teach us to remember. Maybe we should teach everyone through commercials. Just imagine what we could accomplish. It staggers the imagination.

All: Now, what do you really think America is?

Narrator: Mama Mia, it's a spicy meat ball and I need some Alka Seltzer.

118

All: And what does it mean to you?

Narrator: Baseball, Hot dogs, Apple Pie and Chervolet.

Solo 2:   What do we want to do America?

All: (Sung) Plop, plop, fiz, fiz oh what a relief it is.
            Ta Da. (Drop head signaling end of performance)

(NOTE: The singing lends itself to some basic dance or movement by the group to add to the total performance. This can be done by the director.)

Written and produced by Jeff Zwagerman, and the Sibley High School Choral Readers at the All-State Speech Festival at Simpson College.

THE CASUAL APPROACH TO VIOLENCE*
YOU'VE GOT TO BE CAREFULLY TAUGHT

Chorus

> You've got to be taught to hate and fear/
> You've got to be taught from year to year,
> It's got to be drummed in your dear little ear/
> You've got to be carefully taught./
> You've got to be taught to be afraid,
> Of people whose eyes are oddly made,
> And people whose skin is a different shade/
> You've got be carefully taught./
> You've got to be taught before it's too late,
> Before you are six or seven or eight,
> To hate all the people your relatives hate/
> You've got to be carefully taught/
> You've got to be carefully taught./

*Reprinted by permission Mary Gwen Owen, director Macalester College Drama Chorus.

119

Man 1	Hey Ned, did you see the fight Saturday Night?
Man 2	Did I!
Man 1	How was it anyway? Good?
Man 2	Good! Boy you should have seen it! Blood all over that guy.
Man 1	Man, oh, man I thought he'd *never* go down, Joblonski socked him in the head ten times, I bet.
Man 2	And when he went down—He was *out.* . . .
Man 1	You should have heard that crowd roar.
Man 2	I wish I'd seen it. That one last week was no good—technical stuff. Both the guys walked out of the thing fresh as a daisy—
Man 1	You should have heard the crowd boo—
Chorus	The casual living room approach to violence.
Solo	So What! Everyone watches fights and anyway the fighters get paid for it—plenty.
Boy	Mommy, this is the breakfast food I want: Look, see the prizes, Three guided missiles and two jet bombers!
	(Boy and girl out front with cereal box and toy noise maker)
Mother	But Billy, you have a whole set of soldiers and all those airplanes.
Boy	I know, but I don't have any guided missiles or jet bombers, and you can't have a war without guided missiles. Look at this one. I bet I could wipe out the Russians just like that! I bet I could wipe out the whole world—
Mother	Well, I suppose you could, dear. All right, if you take it, remember you'll have to eat all the crackers inside the box too. Otherwise you won't grow to be a big boy.
Boy	Ok—Ok—Ok—Bang! Bang! Bang! (noise maker)
Chorus	The glamorous casual approach to violence.
Narrator 1	
	Or is it casual? Who is it that plans those toys? These prizes? What can we be thinking of? Or are we thinking?

Chorus	Violence—the casual approach to violence.
	One, two, one, two
	Alla ka zoo
	Alla ka zoo
	Rock'em, Sock 'em
	Knock 'em in the head
	Hound 'em, Pound 'em
	Leave 'em for dead.
	One Twooooooo
	Alla Ka Zooooooo
Men	Kill 'em, Kill 'em.
Chorus	The regular fall approach to violence.
Narrator 2	But they are young. Athletics are a good outlet for them.
Chorus	The casual approach to violence.
	The casual, unthinking approach.
All chorus	Is this the way we prepare our children to accept violence?

And when the siren sounds, what do we all do?
We run to the table and lie down under it and put our hands over our faces.
That's right. Who knows why we do this?
So we won't be blown to bits!

This is the way we	*(Three girls run around*
Teach our children	*bench to tune of "Here*
Teach our children	*we go round the Mulberry*
Teach our children	*Bush")*
This is the way we	
Teach our children	
All in a civil defense drill.	

Narrator 2

Blown to bits. . .blown to bits. . .the babies. . .
Our babies. . .Japanese babies. . . African babies
. . .Russian babies. . .Egyptian babies. . .white
babies. . .black babies. . . .

Narrator 1 You've got to fight violence with violence.
You've got to be prepared. You've got to teach
them young how to crouch and cover their
faces. How to yell the words that mean hurt the
other guy first or he'll hurt you. You've got to
soak 'em in blood so they'll be ready—Give 'em

	guns with their baby food so they'll be prepared when the time comes.
Chorus	The casual approach...No use frightening them all of a sudden.
Chorus	Get them used to it.
Narrator 2	The Son of God goes forth to war....
Men	Onward Christian Soliders
Sing	Marching as to war...
Chorus	Rockets red glare
	The bombs bursting in...
Narrator 1	I still say we've got to
	Keep them ready
	Keep them prepared
	No need to jolt them
	Just keep them prepared.
Narrator 2	Prepared? Prepared for what?
Narrator 1	For violence?
	Every politician
	Every general
	Every teacher
	Every minister
	Every scientist
	Every government knows that violence is unthinkable.
Chorus	There have always been wars.
Chorus	There will always be wars.
Man	Why?
	Why?...Why??...Why?
Narrator 2	Well—because—because of the Russians!
Narrator 1	Anyway, we've got all those bombs and guided missiles. Why, we can wipe them all out. We can wipe out the whole world.
Chorus louder	The whole world
each	The whole world
time	The whole world
Narrator 2	And when we wipe out the whole world, what of us?
Narrator 1	What of our children? What of our children's children?
Chorus	Well, so we don't wipe out us. We've got to be prepared anyway.

122

Chorus	The casual approach is the best approach.
Narrator 2	Yes, prepared—but not for violence—with babies crouching under kindergarten tables, not for breakfast food full of guided missiles—Prepared for living—for knowing—for loving.
Narrator 1	Prepared for ideas.
Narrator 2	What are we afraid of?
Narrator 1	We have nothing to fear but fear itself.
Chorus	The Power Elite will see about that.— *(quickly snap finger)*
Narrator 2	The Hidden Persuaders have taken over?
Chorus	...like a cigarette should.
Narrator 1	That may all be— the People will live on the learning, blundering people with the great bundle of grief upon their shoulders. And overhead a shovelful of stars for keepers shot over with the lights of babies not yet born. There are those that believe that the idea of world law is far more potent than megatons of megatons of megatons.
Narrator 2	So what! Let them have their little United Nations. That will keep them busy. But we've got to meet violence with violence and show the world who's boss. ...If we're prepared with bombs and guided missiles. ..we can't lose—
Chorus sing	onward Christian soliders Marching as to war. ..
Narrator 1	Christians—The greatest Christian of all—The carpenter from Nazareth, went up into the mountain and He spoke so all could hear...
Narrator 2	"Blessed are the meek, for they shall inherit the earth,"
Narrator 1	"Blessed are the merciful, for they shall obtain mercy."
Narrator 2	Blessed are the peacemakers, for they shall be called the children of God."
Narrator 1	It has been said by them of old time, "Thou shalt not kill; and whosoever shall kill shall be in danger of judgment."

Solo sing Women sing	Our God, our help in ages past, Our hope for years to come Oh, beautiful for spacious skies, For amber waves of grain. For purple mountain majesties, Above the fruited plain. America, America, God shed his grace on thee. And crown thy good with brotherhood, From sea to shining sea.
Chorus	Rise up ye men of God, Have done with lesser things. . . Oh brother man Fold to thy heart thy brother Where pity dwells, The peace of God is there. And they shall beat their swords into plowshares And their spears into pruning hooks. Neither shall they learn war, anymore.

Mary Gwen Owen
Director, Drama Choros
Macalester College
St. Paul, Minnesota

THE LONESOME TRAIN*

Narrator   The long war was over. And the tall man with
moves   the sad eyes and the stooping shoulders was
out   tired. And so one night he did what everybody
toward   likes to do sometimes when they're tired. He
front of   went to a show. He went down to Ford's
stage as   Theatre in Washington town and he sat in a box
he speaks   and it was the Number 1 box because he was a
pretty big man.

Well, the play went on, and along about the middle of the evening something happened that wasn't on the program. I guess you all know what that was. The news spread pretty fast. . .

Ballad Singer   *(sings, plays guitar)*
(to front of   They carried the news from Washington
stage   That Abraham Lincoln's time had come;
John Wilkes Booth shot Lincoln Dead,
With a pistol bullet through the head!

Chorus enters   The slaves were free, the war was won,
slowly all but   But the fight for freedom was just begun
Solo No. 7   There were still slaves,
The hungry and poor,
Men were not free to speak.

Freedom's a thing that has no ending,
It needs to be cared for, it needs defending;
A great long job for many hands,
Carrying freedom 'cross the land!

Narrator	A job for all the people, carrying freedom across the land. A job for Lincoln's people! And you know who Lincoln's people were.
Each solo *enter and* *takes place* *on train*	(Solo 1) A Kansas farmer, (Solo 2) a Brooklyn sailor, (Solo 3) an Irish policeman, (Solo 4) a Jewish tailor, (Solo 5) an old storekeeper shaking his head handing over a loaf of bread; (Solo 6) a buffalo hunter telling a story out in the Oregon Territory.
Ballad Singer *remainder* *of chorus* *enters*	They were his people, he was their man, You couldn't quite tell where the people left off, And where Abe Lincoln began. Solo 7 (comes out from group, then returns) There was a silence in Washington town, when they carried Mr. Lincoln down.
Chorus	A lonesome train on a lonesome track,/ seven coaches painted black./ *(move arms, in unison like train)*
Narrator	Mr. Lincoln's funeral train traveling the long road from Washington to Baltimore,
Solo Voice *(call out* *as conductor)*	Baltimore to Philadelphia, Philadelphia to New York Albany, Syracuse, Cleveland, Chicago, to Springfield Illinois.
Chorus	A slow train,/ a quiet train,/ carrying Lincoln home again./
Ballad Singer	It wasn't quite mist,/ it was almost rain, falling down on that funeral train, there was a strange and quiet crowd, nobody wanted to talk out loud. Along the streets, across the square, Lincoln's people were waiting there.

126

Narrator	A young solider stood in the road and said:
Solider	You'd think they'd have warned him
(comes out	
from group)	even a rattlesnake warns you.
Narrator	And an old man answered:
Old Man	This one must have been a copperhead!
(comes out	
from group,	
returns)	
Chorus	A lonesome train on a lonesome track/
(moving arms	seven coaches painted black/
in unison)	they carried Mr. Lincoln down/
	the train started, the wheels went round,/
	you could hear the whistle for miles around,
	crying, *Freedom!* (as train whistles)
	Freedom!
Ballad Singer	They tell a story about that train,
	they say that Lincoln wasn't on that train:
	When that train started on its trip that day,

> *Chorus moves,*
> *and sits on*
> *floor,*
> *back to*
> *audience.*

Lincoln was in Alabama. .

Yes, Sir, down in Alabama (speaks)

> *(Chorus hums "Swing Low*
> *Sweet Chariot" through-*
> *out this verse, swaying*
> *in unison from left to right)*

in an old wooden church, (sing)

didn't have no paint,

didn't have no floor

didn't have no glass in the window

just a pulpit and some wooden benches

Solo	O Great God Almighty, Lord. . (Moan)
	(Amens and ad libs by congregation through
	following sequences)
Ballad Singer	Just a pulpit and some wooden benches,
(speak)	and Mr. Lincoln on the last bench away in

	the back (Mr. Lincoln puts bench down
	stage behind chorus and sits)
	listening to the sermon,
	listening to the singing.
Chorus	
(Softly)	Amen, brother, amen.
Solo	You may bury me in the east,
Negro preacher	
in front of	You may bury me in the west
chorus ex-	But I'll hear the trumpet sound in the
pounds with appro—	
priate gestures.	Morning!

Solo	In the morning, Lord, in the morning!
Preacher	This evening, brothers and sisters,
	I come in the holiest manner, to tell you how he died.
Chorus	He died, yes,/Lord, he's dead!/
Preacher	He was a-lyin' there,
	His blood on the ground,
	covering the ground:
	And while he was lyin' there the sun arose,
	and it recognized him.
	Just as soon as the sun approached him
	it clothed itself in sackcloth and ashes!
	O, went down in the morning!
	(woman) (men)
Chorus	Lord, the sun went down!/ Yes, Lord,
	it went down!
Preacher	He was a lyin' there,
	and the sky turned dark,
	and seven angels leaped over the battlements of
	glory,
	and come down to get him;
	and just when they came near him he rose,
	yes, Lord, he rose up and walked down among us,
	praise God,
	he walked down among his people!
Solo (Woman)	Lord, He's living now!
Preacher	We got a new land; my dear friends, we got a new land
	Ain't no riding boss with a whip. *(no)* Chorus
	Don't have no backbiters, *(no)* Chorus

	liars can't go, cheaters can't go,
	ain't no separate kingdom
	no high sheriff to bring us back!
Solo (Woman)	We got a new land!
Preacher	You may bury me in the east,
	you may bury me in the west,
	but I'll hear the trumpet sound in the morning!
Chorus	In the morning, Lord,/ in the morning!
Ballad Singer	Down in Alabama, (speak)

nothing but a pulpit and some wooden benches,
and Mr. Lincoln sitting in the back   *Chorus returns*
away in the back.   *to original*
                                           train position
                                           on benches

Chorus	A lonesome train on a lonesome track,/
	seven coaches painted black;/
	a slow train, a quiet train,
	carrying Lincoln home again./
	Solo Solo Solo
Solo Voices	Washington, Baltimore, Harrisburg,
	Solo
	Philadelphia. . .(call out as conductor)
Chorus	Coming into New York Town./
	You could hear the whistle for miles around,
	Free-dom!
Narrator	From Washington to New York people lined the
	tracks.
Ballad Singer	A strange crowd, (sing)
	A quiet crowd;
	Nobody wanting to talk out loud.
Narrator	At lonely country crossroads there were farmers
	and their wives and kids standing around for hours;
	in Philadelphia, the line of mourners ran three miles;
	and most of them were deep in mourning;
	an old lady stood by the coffin and said:
Solo	Mr. Lincoln, are you dead? Are you really
	dead? (lady with shawl moves out from chorus to front)
Narrator	And some wanted him dead for a long time.

Chorus	For there were those who cursed the Union those who wanted the people apart,/ while the sound of freedom guns still echoed, Copperheads struck at the people's heart./
Ballad Singer	(speak) I've heard it said that when that train pulled into New York Town, Mr. Lincoln wasn't around, (sings) He was where there was work to be done, where there were people having fun; When that funeral train pulled into New York ...Lincoln was down in a Kansas town, swinging his lady round and round! (speak) He was back in New Salem with his boyhood sweetheart. Back with Ann Rutledge whom he loved with all his heart.
Solo	Out of me unworthy and unknown. The vibrations of deathless music. With malice toward none, with charity for all. Out of me the forgiveness of millions toward millions, and the beneficent face of a nation shining with justice and truth. I am Ann Rutledge who sleeps beneath these weeds, beloved in the life of Abraham Lincoln, wedded to him. Not through union but through separation. Bloom forever, O Republic, from the dust of my bosom! (Lincoln exits to get beard)
Solo	*Solo* Pretty little gal, around she goes, swing your lady for a do-si-do! First to the right, and then to the left, and then to the gal that you love best! Duck for the oyster, dig for the clam, pass right through to the promised land!

*Call as a square
dance caller
4 couples run out
from chorus to
dance. Chorus
claps hands in
rhythm*

130

Chorus	Those Kansas boys didn't have a chance,	*(dancers*
	when young Abe Lincoln came to dance!/	*return to*
	A lonesome train on a lonesome track,/	*chorus*
	seven coaches painted black,/	*position)*
	The train started, the wheel went round,	
	on the way to Cleveland town,/	

     solo   *solo*   *solo* *solo* *solo*

         Poughkeepsie, Albany, Utica, Syracuse, Cleveland. . .
         You could hear the whistle for miles around,/
         Freedom!
         Crying / freedom!   *Chorus leaves benches and moves*
                           around as a crowd to hide
                           Lincoln's entrance. Lincoln enters

Narrator	In Cleveland the crowds were there,
	two hundred and fifty came from Meadville,
	Pennsylvania;
Solo	Five hundred with two brass bands from
	Detroit,
Solo	A million people came from northern Ohio,
	they came to mourn,
	and some went to celebrate.
Ballad Singer	(speaking) Some in the north and some in the west,
	and some by the President's side
	cursed him every day that he lived,
	and cheered the day he died!
Narrator	The copperheads. .
	A New York politician who didn't like Lincoln. . .
	An Ohio businessman who didn't like Negroes. . .
	A Chicago newspaper editor who didn't like people. . .
Girl Alto	*(sing softly)*
	You couldn't quite tell where the people left off
	And where Abe Lincoln began.
Narrator	Naturally the Copperheads went home to celebrate.
Ballad Singer	When that train rolled into Cleveland town

        Mr. Lincoln wasn't around;   *Crowds moves*
        Lincoln sat in a hospital ward,   *behind Lincoln*
        far from the funeral train,   *to audience.*
        trying to quiet a soldier's pain.

Lincoln	(speaks throughout)
	Do you mind if I stand by the side
	of the bed? *(Soldier sits on bench*
	with bandage or arm in sling)
	Lincoln stands behind him.
Soldier	No, sir.
Lincoln	Where were you wounded, son?
Soldier	At Bull Run, sir, and Chancellorsville,
	I was shot when we stormed the hill;
	And I've been worried since Chancellorsville,
	About killing sir, it's wrong to kill.
Lincoln	I admit, son, that's been bothering me:
	How to make the war and the word agree.
	(Solider takes
	his place in
	chorus).
Chorus	Quiet and tall by the side of the bed. . .
Lincoln	There is a reason.
Chorus	There is a reason,/ Lincoln said.
Lincoln	Until all men are equal, and all are free
	There will be no peace.
	While there are whips and chains,
	And men to use them,
	There will be no peace;
	After the battles,
	After the blood and wounded,
	When the chains are smashed,
	And the whips are broken,
	And the men who held the whips are dead!
	When men are brothers and men are free,
	The killing will end, the war will cease,
	When free men have a free men's peace!
Ballad Singer	(speaks) I'll be going home, soon, the soldier said.
	Lincoln turned from the side of the bed.
Lincoln	I'll see you there.
Ballad Singer	I'll see you there, Mr. Lincoln said.
Chorus	A slow train,/ a funeral train,/
	Carrying Lincoln home again./ *(Speaking)*
	(arms imitating
	train in basic position)

Conductor	Last stop! Springfield, Illinois!
Narrartor	Lincoln's neighbors came,
	Farmers from over in the next county,
	Shopkeepers and shoemakers,
	Men who'd hired him for a lawyer,
	Men who'd split rails with him:
	They came from Mattoon and Salem,
	Fellows who'd swapped stories with
	Abe Lincoln during those long Illinois
	winter nights;
	Lincoln's neighbors were there./
Chorus	A slow train,/ a warm rain,/
	Falling down on the funeral train,/
	(While the sound of the freedom *(faster)*
	guns still echoed,
	Copperheads struck at the people's heart!)/
Ballad Singer	(speaking) When that train pulled into
	Springfield, you know where Lincoln was?
	He was standing with his friends in the
	back of the crowd!
	Yes, sir!
Chorus and	Standing tall,/ standing proud,/
Ballad Singer	Wearing a shawl instead of a shroud!?
Ballad Singer	(speaking) Abe Lincoln was with his
	friends, telling jokes!

Lincoln places single bench or stool at back of crowd and appears above the crowd

(Chorus hums behind) *(Battle Hymn of the Republic)*

Lincoln	I presume you all know who I am. I am humble
	Abraham Lincoln. My politics are short and sweet,
	like the old woman's dance.

man from chorus faces Lincoln

Man	Mr. Lincoln, isn't it right that some men
	should be masters and some should be slaves?
Lincoln	Brother, if God intended some men to do all
	the work and no eating, He would have made
	some men with all hands and no mouths.

133

Chorus	Standing tall,/ standing proud./

*girl
from chorus
faces Lincoln*

Woman	Well, I say, America for Americans. What happens on the other side of the ocean shouldn't be any skin off our backs. Right, Mr. Lincoln?
Lincoln	Well, I'll tell you, ma'am. It seems to me that the strongest bond of human sympathy, outside your family of course, should be the one uniting all working people, of all nations, tongues and kindreds.
Chorus	Wearing a shawl instead of a shroud./
Woman	Somehow, I wouldn't expect the President of the United States to be such a common man.

*from chorus
faces Lincoln*

Lincoln	I think God must have loved the common people— He made so many of them.
Chorus	Wearing a shawl instead of a shroud.
Child	Mr. Lincoln, how does it feel to be President?

*child from
chorus faces Lincoln*

Lincoln	Well, now; it feels sort of like the fellow that ran out of town on a rail. If it wasn't for the honor of it, I'd just as soon walk.
Ballad Singer	(singing) They were his people, he was their man you couldn't quite tell where the people left off, and where Abe Lincoln began.
Chorus	A lonesome train on a lonesome track,/ Seven coaches painted black./
Ballad Singers	(speaking) Abe Lincoln had an Illinois face,

134

And he came out of a pioneer race;
He knew how hard the fight would be
But he liked the idea of being free.
His heart was tough as a railroad tie,
He was made of stuff that doesn't die;
He was made of hopes, he was made of fears,
He was made to last a million years!
Freedom's a thing that has no ending.
It needs to be cared for, it needs defending!
Free-dom!

Millard Lampell

Lonesome Train is one of the most effective choric dramas to be presented by a group. It is appropriate for many occasions and plays twenty minutes. The ballad singer should have a pleasing voice and be skillful with a guitar. The narrator holds the piece together and should be a sensitive, articulate interpreter. Any number may be used in the chorus. Quite detailed instructions for movement and costuming are given to you for this number. You need not be bound by them.

From the Bible

Some of the world's most dramatic literature can be found in the Bible. Here is an excellent opportunity to worship with drums, harps, flutes, tympanies, and dance, as well as with the word. I am including only a few examples, but I am sure you will think of others. For example, try the inspiring story of Moses, "Let My People Go."

COLOSSIANS 3

An adaptation prepared especially for the Northwestern College Choral Readers by Cheryl Peters Cornelder.

Chorus	Since you became alive again so to speak,/ when Christ arose
	from the dead,/Now set your sights on the rich treasures and joys awaiting you in heaven/
	Where Christ sits behind God
	upon the right hand of God
	in the place of honor and power.
Solo	Set your affection on things above
Chorus	on things above.
(echo)	Not on things of the earth.
	Let heaven fill your thoughts
	think, meditate upon great things.
	For you are dead,/ and your life is hid with Christ in God./
	When Christ, who is our life, shall appear/, then shall you also appear with him in glory/
	You will shine with Him
Chorus	and glisten in His glory.
commanding	
tone Solo:	Put away worldly sins.
	Fornication, uncleanliness, lust and evil desires/
	Coveting the riches of this life/, which is idolatry./
	For God's wrath, the anger of our great God,
Chorus	Will fall on those who disobey./
	on those who do these things./
Solo	You used to do those things when your life was still
men *(softly)*	part of this world/

136

Solo	But now is the time to cast off these impure garments/,
Women	The garments of anger,/ the garments of hatred/
	The garments of cursing/, and those of filthy language./
Chorus	You must not lie to one another,/
Solo	For it was in your old nature you did these things.
Men	You now have put off the old man and his deed.

chorus

And you have a new man,/ a new Nature,

Solo	A new kind of life that is ever learning more and
Men	more. . . .

chorus

Of what is right,/ of what is good,/
and imitating the life of Christ who gave you this new
man.

Men	/In Him/, and in your new life/, it is not important whether

m 5   m 6   w 6

a man is Greek/ or Jew/ or circumcised/

w 7   w 7   w 8   w 9

or uncircumcised/ or black/ or red/ or yellow/

w 8   w 9   w 10

his race/ nor his nationality/ nor his education/
all women

nor his social position will be important to you./

all men

Solo	For Christ will be all/ to all/ and in all/.
Men	Therefore put on the elements of
	tenderhearted pity and kindness to others/.
	Be humble of mind/, if any man have a quarrel against

chorus   Solo women   chorus

you,/ forgive him./ Even as Christ forgave you,/ so do
also you forgive.

Chorus	And above all these things
Solo	Put on the garment of love
Men	
Chorus	This is the bond of perfectness/
	Let the peace of God rule in your hearts./
Solo	This is your privilege/ and always be thankful/
Women	
Solo	Let the word of Christ dwell in you richly/

Women	*Chorus*
	In all wisdom;
	woman 10 *woman 11*
Women	Teaching and admonishing one another/ in Psalms/
	woman 12
	and hymns
	Chorus
	and spiritual song/ singing with grade in your hearts
	to the Lord/
	And whatever you do
	in word/ or in deed. *Solo men*
Chorus	Do it heartily/ as you are doing it for the Lord
Chorus	Not for men!
	And you shall know that from the Lord
	you shall receive a reward/
Solo Men	A great payment,
Solo Women	For you are serving the Lord Jesus/
Solo Men	And his inheritance you shall receive
Chorus	*You shall receive.*

ECCLESIASTES III

	To everything there is a season, and a time
	to every
	purpose under the heaven
Solo	A time to be born, and a time to die;
Solo	A time to plant, and a time to pluck up that which is
	planted;
Solo	A time to kill, and a time to heal;
Solo	A time to break down and a time to build up;
Solo	A time to weep, and a time to laugh;
Solo	A time to mourn, and a time to dance;
Solo	A time to cast away stones, and a time to gather
	stones together;
Solo	A time to embrace, and a time to refrain from
	embracing;
Solo	A time to get, and a time to lose;
Solo	A time to keep, and a time to cast away;
Solo	A time to read, and a time to sew;
Solo	A time to keep silence, and a time to speak;

Solo	A time to love, and a time to hate;
Solo	A time of peace, and a time of war;
Chorus	To everything there is a season, and a time to every purpose under the heaven.

Bible

ECCLESIASTES XII

Remember also thy Creator
in the days of thy youth,
before the evil days come,
and the years draw nigh/when thou shalt say/
I have no pleasure in them;/
before the sun and the light, and the moon, and
  the stars are darkened,/
and the clouds return after the rain;/
in the day when the keepers of the house shall
  tremble,/
and the strong men shall bow themselves,/
and the girders shall cease because they are few,
and those that look out of the windows shall be
  darkened,/
and the doors shall be shut in the street;/
when the sound of the grinding is low,
and one shall rise at the voice of a bird,
and all the daughters of music shall be brought
  low:/
yea/ they shall be afraid of that which is high/
and terrors shall be in the way/
and the almond-tree shall blossom,/
and the grasshopper shall be a burden,/
and desire shall fail;/
because man goeth to his everlasting home,
and the mourners go about the streets:/
before the silver cord is loosed,
or the golden bowl is broken,/
or the pitcher is broken at the fountain,/
or the wheel broken at the cistern,/
and the dust returneth to the earth as it was,/

and the spirit returneth unto God,/
who gave it./

I love this—it is so musical. If you want to work hard it would be beautiful as a solo—with musical background—and using the sticks.   (Your stick choir) It needs much *dynamics.*

THE FIERY FURNACE
Daniel 3:1-28,30 (KJV)

(drum)

Chorus   Nebuchadnezzar the king made an image of gold,
             whose height was threescore cubits,/
         and the breadth thereof six cubits:/
         he set it up in the plain of Dura, in the province
             of Babylon./
         Then Nebuchadnezzar the king sent to gather together

Keep   *solo*
voices   the princes,/
up   *solo*   *solo*   *solo*
         the governors,/ and the captains,/ the judges,/ the
                 solo
             treasures,/
                 solo   *solo*   *Chorus*
         the counselors,/ the sheriffs,/ and all the rulers
             of the provinces,/
         to come to the dedication of the image which
         Nebuchadnezzar the king had set up./
         When they were all gathered together they stood
             before the image Nebuchadnezzar had set up/.
         Then a herald cried aloud/ (drums)

Solo   To you it is commanded, O people, nations, and
             languages,
         That at what time you hear the sound of the cornet,
             flute, harp, sackbut, psaltery, dulcimer,
             and all kinds of music, (cymbals)
         ye fall down and worship the golden image
         that Nebudchadnezzar the king hath set up:
         And whoso falleth not down and worshippeth shall
             the same hour   *drums*
         be cast into the midst of a burning/fiery/furnace./

140

Women	Therefore, at that time, when all the people
	heard the sound of the cornet,/flute,/harp./sackbut,/
	    psaltery,/ and all kinds of music,/
	all the people,/the nations,/and the languages
	fell down and worshipped the golden image that
	    Nebuchadnezzar the king had set up/.
	Wherefore at that time certain Chaldeans came
	    near, and accused the Jews./
	They spake and said to the king Nebuchadnezzar,

Men	O king, live for ever,/
	Thou, O king, hast made a decree, that every man
	that shall hear all kinds of music shall fall
	    down and worship the golden image/:
	And whoso falleth not down and worshippeth,
	that he should be cast into the midst of a
	    burning/fiery/furnance,/ (drums)
	There are certain Jews whom thou hast set over
	the affairs of the province of Babylon/, Shadrach/,
	    Meshack,/ and Abednego;/
	these men, O king, have not regarded thee:/
	they serve not thy gods,/
	nor worship the golden image which thou has set up./

Chorus	Then Nebuchadnezzar in his rage and fury commanded to bring Shadrach,/ Meshach,/ and Abednego./ Then he brought these men before the king./ Nebuchadnezzar spake and said unto them./

Solo
another man
	Is it true, O Shadrach, Meshach, and Abednego?
	do not ye serve my gods,/ nor worship the golden
	    image which I have set up?/
	Now if ye be ready at what time ye hear the sound
	    of the cornet, (cymbals)
	flute,/harp,/sackbut/, psaltery/, and dulcimer/, and
	all kinds of music,/ ye fall down and worship the
	    image which I have made;/ *well:*
	But if ye worship not,/ ye shall be cast the same
	hour into the midst of a burning/fiery/furnace;/(drums)
	and who is that God that shall deliver you out of
	    my hands?/

Chorus	Shadrach,/Meshack,/and Abednego,/ answered and said to the king/

Men	O Nebuchadnezzar,/ we are not careful to answer

Men   O Nebuchadnezzar,/ we are not careful to answer
thee in this matter./
If it be so/, our God whom we serve is able
to deliver us from burning/fiery/furnace/, (drums)
and he will deliver us out of thine hand, O king./
But if not,/ be it known unto thee, o king,
that we will not serve thy gods,/
nor worship the golden image which thou hast set up./

Chorus   Then was Nebuchadnezzar full of fury/,
(louder)   and the form of his visage was changed
against Shadrach,/Meshach,/ and Abednego:/
therefore he spake and commanded that they
    should heat the furnace
one seven times more than it was wont to be
    heated./

Softer   And he commanded the most mighty men that were
in his army to bind Shadrach,/Meshach,/and Abednego/,
and to cast them into the burning/fiery/furnace./ (drums)
Then these men were bound in their coats/, their
    hose,/and their hats,/ and their other garments,/
and were cast into the midst of the burning fiery
    furnace. (drums)
Therefore because the king's commandment was
    urgent,
and the fire exceedingly hot,/the flame of the
fire slew those men that took up Shadrach,/Meshach,/
    and Abednego,/
And these three men fell down bound into the midst
    of the burning/fiery/furnace./
Then Nebuchadnezzar the king was astonished and
    rose up in haste;
and spake, and said unto his counselors,/

Men   Did we not cast three men bound into the midst of
2   the fire?
                                   men

Chorus   They answered and said unto the king, true, o
           king.   *men 2*

Chorus   He answered and said, Lo, I see four men loose,
walking in the midst of the fire, and they have no
hurt; (and the form of the fourth is like the Son
    of God.)

Chorus	Then Nebuchadnezzar came near to the mouth of the burning/fiery/furnace,/and spake,/and said/ (drums) Shadrach,/Meshach,/and Abednego,/ ye servants of the most high God, come forth and come hither./ Then Shadrach/,Meshach,/and Abednego/, came forth of the midst of the fire. And the princes/,governors,/and captains/,and the king's counselors,/being gathered together, saw these men upon whose bodies the fire had no power,/ nor was a hair of their head singed/, neither were their coats changed, nor the smell of fire had passed on them./ Then Nebuchadnezzar spake and said, Blessed be the God of Shadrach,/Meshach, and Abednego,/
Men 2	who hath sent his angel, and delivered his servants that trusted in him, and have changed the king's word, and yielded their bodies, that they might not serve nor worship any god, except their own God.
Chorus	Then the king promoted Shadrach,/Meshach,/and Abednego,/ in the province of Babylon./

(Use two dancers in leotards and tunics with finger cymbals. Use drums and cymbals and lighting effects if possible.)

THE GLORY OF THE LORD

Group 1	Great and marvellous are thy works, Lord God Almighty (Rev. 15:3b)
Group 2	Just and true are they ways, thou King of Saints. (Rev. 15:3c)
Group 1	Who shall fear thee, O Lord, and glorify thy name? For thou art holy.
Group 2	For all nations shall come and worship before thee.
Group 1	For whosoever shall call upon the name of the Lord shall be saved. (Romans 10:13)

Group 2	How then shall they call on him in whom they have not believed? (Romans 10:14a)
Group 1	And how shall they believe in him of whom they have not heard? (Romans 10:14b)
Group 2	And how shall they hear without a preacher (Romans 10:14c)
Group 1	And how shall they preach, except they be sent? (Romans 10:15a)
Chorus	As it is written,/ How beautiful upon the mountains are the feet of him that bringeth good tidings,/ that publisheth peace;/ that bringeth good tidings of good, that publisheth salvation;/ that saith unto Zion,/ Thy God reigneth!/ (Isaiah 52:7)

Two groups speak antiphonally

THE PRODIGAL SON*

rhythm snaps

Chorus	Young man—young man/young man *fast women / slow women*
	man Young man—
Chorus	Your arm's too short to box with God.
Solo 1	But Jesus spake in a parable, and he said:
Solo 2	A certain man had two sons,/two sons *Chorus*
Solo 1	Jesus didn't call this man a name,/no name *chorus*
Solo 1	But his name is God Almighty./ God Almighty *Chorus*
Solo 1	And Jesus didn't call these sons by name,
Solo 1	But ev'ry young man,/ every man *chorus*
Solo 1	Ev'rywhere,/ everywhere *Chorus*
Solo 1	Is one of these two sons.

*From *God's Trombones* by James Weldon Johnson, Copyright 1927 by the Viking Press, Inc.,© renewed 1955 by Grace Nail Johnson. Reprinted by permission of the Viking Press.

Chorus	And the younger son said to his father,
	Solo 3
	He said:/Father, divide up the property,
	And give me my portion now.
	Solo 4
Chorus	And the father with tears in his eyes said:/Son,
	Don't leave your father's house.
Men	But the boy was stubborn in his head,
Women	And haughty in his heart.
Chorus	And he took his share of his father's goods,
	And went into a far-off country./
Men	There comes a time,
Women	There comes a time
Chorus	When ev'ry young man looks out from his father's house,
	Longing for the far-off country./
	And the young man journeyed on his way,
	And he said to himself as he traveled along,/
Solo 3	This sure is an easy road,
	Nothing like the rough forrows behind my father's plow.
Men	Young man—
Women	Young man—
Chorus	Smooth and easy is the road
	women
Chorus	That leads to hell and destruction/hell and destruction
speaks in	The further you travel, the faster you go.
fast	No need to trudge and sweat and toil,
rhythm	Just slip and slide and slip and slide
	Till you bang up against hell's iron gate. (clap hands)
Solo	And the younger son kept travelling along.
	Till at night-time he came to a city.
	And the city was bright in the night-time like day,
	The streets all crowded with people,
	Brass bands and string bands a-playing,
	And ev'rywhere the young man turned
	There was singing and laughing and dancing.
	And he stopped a passer-by and he said:
Solo 3	Tell me what city this is?

145

Solo 5

	And the passer-by laughed and said;/Don't you know?
	This is Babylon, Babylon,
rhythm	That great city of Babylon.
	Come on, my friend, and go along with me.
Chorus	And the young man joined the crowd.
Men	Young man—
Women	Young man—(slow)
Chorus	You're never lonesome in Babylon.
	You can always join a crowd in Babylon
Men	Young man—
Women	Young man—(fast)
Chorus	You can never be alone in Babylon, (stop rhythm)
Solo	Alone with your Jesus in Babylon.

rhythm snaps (Women–Men)

solo 7

Solo 6	You can never find a place,/a lonesome place,/
Solo 6	A lonesome place to go down on your knees,
	And talk with your God, in Babylon.
Chorus	You're always in a crowd in Babylon. (rhythm)
Solo 1	And the young man went with his new-found friend,
	And bought himself some brand new clothes,
Men	And he spent his days in the drinking dens,
	Swallowing the fires of hell.
Women	And he spent his nights in the gambling dens,
	Throwing dice with the devil for his soul.
Solo 1	And he met up with the women of Babylon.
Men	Oh, the women of Babylon!
Solo	Dressed in yellow and purple and scarlet,
1	Loaded with rings and earrings and bracelets,
	Their lips like a honeycomb dripping with honey,
	Perfumed and sweet-smelling like a jasmine flower;
	And the jasmine smell of the Babylon women
	Got in his nostrils and went to his head,
	And he wasted his substance in riotous living/(Pause)

men

Chorus	In the evening,/in the black and dark of night/
Chorus	With the sweet-sinning women of Babylon.
Men	And they stripped him of his money,

rhythm	And they stripped him of his clothes,
	And they left him broke and ragged
	In the streets, in the streets, in the streets of Babylon.
Solo 1	Then the young man joined another crowd—
Chorus	The beggars and lepers of Babylon.
Solo	And he went to feeding swine,
1	And he was hungrier than the hogs;
	He got down on his belly in the mire and mud
	And ate the husks with the hogs.
	And not a hog was too low to turn up his nose
Men	At the man/in the mire/of Babylon./
Chorus	Then the young man came to himself—
Women	He came to himself and said:
Solo 3	In my father's house are many mansions,
	Ev'ry servant in his house has bread to eat,
	I will arise and go to my father.
Men	And his father saw him afar off,
Women	And he ran up the road to meet him.
Men	He put clean clothes upon his back,
Women	And a golden chain around his neck,
Chorus	He had a feast and killed the fatted calf,
	And invited the neighbors in.
Men	Oh-o-sinner
	When you're mingling with the crowd in Babylon—
	Drinking the wine of Babylon—
rhythm	Running with the women of Babylon—
snaps	You forget about God, and you laugh at Death.
fast	Today you've got the strength of a bull in your neck
	And the strength of a bear in your arms,
	But some o' these days, some o' these days,
	You'll have a hand-to-hand struggle with bony Death
	And Death is bound to win.

rhythm snaps	Young man, young man come away from Babylon
	That hell-border city of Babylon.
	Leave the dancing and gambling of Babylon,
	The wine and whiskey of Babylon,
	The hot-mouthed women of Babylon;

Solo	Fall down on your knees,
Solo	And say in your heart:
Chorus	I will arise/and go to my Father.

SONG OF LOVE

From I Corinthians 13 and the Song of Solomon

This song of love can be used for many occasions. It even is appropriate for a wedding.

Chorus	Set me as a seal upon thine heart;
	As a seal upon thine arm;
Women	For love is strong as death;
Men	Jealousy is cruel as the grave;
Women	The flashes thereof are flashes of fire,
Chorus	A very flame of the Lord,
Women	Many waters cannot quench love,
Men	Neither can the floods drown it:
Chorus	If a man would give all the substance of his house for love,
	It would utterly be condemned,
Solo 1	If I speak with the tongues of men and of angels but have not love, I am become sounding brass, of a clanging cymbal.
Solo 2	And if I have the gift of prophecy, and know all mysteries and all knowledge; and if I have all faith, so as to remove mountains, but have not love, I am nothing.
Solo	And if I bestow all my goods to feed the poor, and if I give my body to be burned, but have not love, it profiteth me nothing.

Woman	Love suffereth long, and is kind;
Men	Love envieth not;
Chorus	Love vaunteth not itself, it not puffed up.
	doth not behave itself unseemly,
	seeketh not its own,
	is not provoked,
	taketh no account of evil;
	rejoiceth not in unrighteousness,
	but rejoiceth in the truth.
Solo 4	For now we see in a mirror darkly; but then face to
	face: now I know in part; but then shall I
	know even as also I am known.
Chorus	But now abideth faith, hope, love, these three; and
	the greatest of these is love.
	Eat, o friends
	Drink, yes, drink abundantly of love.

PSALMS

Many of the Biblical Psalms may be used effectively. In fact, an entire program of Psalms is lovely and inspirational. Group them to make an appropriate theme, for instance Psalms 42,84, and 46 may be presented as Psalms of Peace. There are many Psalms of Praise. How appropriate this would be for a Thanksgiving service. You will discover other themes. You may want to send for *The New 23rd* from the Billy Graham film "His Land." Order from Lexicon Music, Inc.

PSALM 8*

Chorus	O Lord, our Lord, how majestic is thy name in
	all the
	earth/
	Thou whose glory above the heavens is chanted by the
	mouth of babes and infants/

*From the Revised Standard Version of the Bible. Copyrighted 1946,1952 © 1971, 1972.

Solo	Thou has founded a bulwark because of thy foes,/to still the enemy and the avenger/ When I look at the heavens, the work of thy fingers, the moon and the stars which thou hast established; What is man that thou art mindful of him, and the son of man that thou doest care for him? Yet, thou hast made him less than God, and doest crown him with glory and honor. Thou hast given him dominion over the works of thy hands; Thou has put all things under his feet—all sheep and oxen, and also the beasts of the field; The birds of the air, and the fish of the sea, whatever passes along the paths of the sea.
Chorus	Oh Lord, our Lord, how majestic is thy name in all the earth!?

Revised Standard Edition

23rd PSALM

Chorus	The Lord is my Pace-setter, I shall not rush,/ He makes me stop and rest for quiet intervals./ He provides me with images of stillness, Which restore my serenity/ He leads me in the ways of efficiency through calmness of mind./ And his guidance is peace./ Even though I have a great many things to accomplish each day, I will not fret/for His presence is here./ His timelessness/His all-importance/ will keep me in balance/ He prepares refreshment and renewal in the midst of my activity/

By anointing my mind with His oils of
    tranquility/
My cup of joyous energy overflows./
Surely harmony and effectiveness shall
    be the fruits of my hours,
For I shall walk in the pace of my Lord,/
    and dwell in His house forever./

Careful phrasing gives this adaptation variety. Read calmly
and smoothly.

AN INDIAN VERSION OF THE TWENTY-THIRD PSALM

Chorus

The Great Father above a Shepherd is/ I am His and with Him I want not./ He throws out to me a rope, and the name of the rope is Love and He draws me to where the grass is green and the water not dangerous,/ and I eat and lie down and am satisfied./

Solo

Sometimes my heart is very weak and falls down but He lifts me up again and draws me into a good road.

Chorus

His name is "Wonderful." Sometimes/ it may be very soon/it may be a long, long, time,/ He will draw me into a valley./ It is dark there, but I'll draw back not/I'll be afraid not/ for it is in between those mountains that the Shepherd Chief will meet me/ and the hunger that I have in my heart all through this life will be satisifed./ Sometimes He makes the love rope into a whip, but afterwards He give me a staff to lean upon./ He spreads a table before me with all kinds of foods. He put His hand upon my head and all the "tired" is gone./ My cup He fills till it runs over./

Solo

What I tell is true, I lie not.

Chorus

These roads that are "away ahead" will stay with me through this life,/ and after/ and afterwards I will go to live in the Big Tepee/ and sit down with the Shepherd Chief forever./

PSALM 24*

This number may be used as a processional.

Chorus *at back* *of room*	The earth is the Lord's and the fullness thereof; the world and they that dwell therein. For he hath founded it upon the seas, and established it upon the floods.
Male *soloist* *on stage*	Who shall ascend unto the hill of the Lord? or who shall stand in his holy place?
Chorus *approaching* *stage*	He that hath clean hands and a pure heart; who hath not lifted up his soul unto vanity, nor sworn deceitfully. He shall receive the blessing from the Lord, and righteousness from the God of his salvation.
Men	This is the generation of them that seek him, that seek thy face, O Jacob.
Chorus	Lift up your heads, O ye gates, and be ye lifted up, ye everlasting doors; and the King of glory shall come in.
Solo	Who is the King of glory?
Men	The Lord strong and mighty, the Lord mighty in battle.
Chorus *on stage*	Lift up your heads, O ye gates; even lift them up, ye everlasting doors; the king of glory shall come in.
Solo	Who is this king of glory?
Chorus	The Lord of hosts, he is the king of glory.

*From the Revised Standard Version of the Bible. Copyrighted 1846,1952,©1971, 1972.

PSALM 34*

Chorus	I will bless the Lord at all times;
	his praise shall continually be in my mouth/
L w	My soul makes its boast in the Lord;
d w	let the afflicted hear and be glad.
L m	O magnify the Lord with me,
Chorus	and let us exalt his name together!
Solo	I sought the Lord and he answered me,
	and delivered me from all my fears./
Solo	Look at him, and be radiant;
	so your faces shall never be ashamed.

solo

d m	The poor man cried,/ and the Lord heard him,
	and saved him out of all his troubles.
L m	The angel of the Lord encamps
	around those who fear him,/and delivers them./
Chorus	O taste and see that the Lord is good!
Solo	Happy is the man who takes refuge in him!
Chorus	O fear the Lord, you his saints/
	for those who fear him/have no want!
Solo	Come, O sons, listen to men,
	I will teach you the fear of the Lord,
	What man is there who desires life,
	and covets many days that he may enjoy good?
	Keep your tongues from evil, and your lips from
	speaking deceit.
	Depart from evil, and do good; seek peace and pursue it.

Revised Standard Version

PSALM 42*

Solo

As a hart longs for flowing streams,
so longs my soul for thee, O God.
My soul thirsts for God, for the living God.
When shall I come and behold the face of God?
My tears have been my food day and night,
while men say to me continually
"Where is your God?"

Solo

These things I remember as I pour out my soul
how I went with the throng and led them in
procession to the house of God
with glad shouts and songs of thanksgiving
a multitude keeping festival.

Chorus

Why are you cast down O my soul/
and why are you disquieted within me?/
Hope in God/ for I shall again praise him
my help and my God./

Solo

By day the Lord commands his steadfast love
and at night his song is with me
a prayer to the God of my life.
I say to God my rock: "Why hast thou forgotten
me? Why go I mourning because of the oppression
of the enemy?"
As a deadly wound in my body my adversaries taunt
me while they say to me continually "Where is
your God?"

Chorus

Why are you cast down O my soul/and why are you
disquieted within me?/
Hope in God/ for I shall again praise him
my help and my God/

Revised Standard Version

PSALM 46*

Chorus	God is our refuge and strength,
(soft)	a very present help in trouble./
build	Therefore we will not fear though
	the earth should change/though the
	mountains shake in the heart of the sea,/
	though its waters roar and foam/though
	the mountains tremble with its tumult./
	drums *cymbals*
softly	There is a river whose streams make
	glad the city of God/
	the holy habitation of the Most High/
	God is in the midst of her, she shall not
	be moved;
	God will help her right early/
build	The nations rage/the kingdoms totter/
	drums *cymbals*
	Come behold the works of the Lord,
	how he has wrought desolations in the earth.
	He makes wars cease to the end of the earth;
	he breaks the bow, and shatters the spear,
climax	he burns the chariots with fire!
soft	"Be still, and know that I am God./
	I am exalted among the nations,
	I am exalted in the earth."/
	The Lord of Hosts is with us;/
climax	the God of Jacob is our refuge./
	drums *cymbals*

—The Bible
Revised Standard Version

Careful dynamics make this selection effective.

PSALM 84*

l w	How lovely is thy dwelling place, O Lord of hosts/My soul longs,/yea faints for the courts of
	_{d w} the Lord/ my heart and flesh sing for joy to the
	_{lm & lw} living God. Even the sparrow finds a home, and
	_{Men} the swallow a nest for herself,/where she may lay her young/, at thy altars,/O Lord of hosts, my king and my God./
Chorus	Blessed are those who dwell in thy house, ever singing thy praise!/
Men	Blessed are the men whose strength is in thee,/in whose heart are the highways to Zion./
l w	As they go through the valley of Baca they make
	_{d w} it a place of springs/the early rain also covers it
	_{lw & dw} with pools/They go from strength to strength—
	_{chorus} the God of gods will be seen in Zion./O Lord God of hosts, hear my prayer;/give ear, O God of Jacob!/
Men	Behold our child, O God/look upon the face of thine anointed/
Chorus	For a day in thy courts is better than a thousand
	_{Solo Men} elsewhere./ I would rather be a doorkeeper in the house of my God than dwell in the tents of wickedness.
l w	For the Lord God is a sun and shield;
d w	He bestows favor and honor.
l w & d w	No good thing does the Lord withhold, from those who walk uprightly.
Chorus	O Lord of hosts, blessed is the man who trusts in thee!

Revised Standard Version

*From the Revised Standard Version of the Bible. Copyrighted 1946,1952. © 1971, 1972.

Music background is effective, Read smoothly and peace-fully.

PSALM 90*

Chorus	Lord, thou hast been our dwelling place in all generations
Man 1	Before the mountains were brought forth
Man 2	or ever thou hadst formed the earth and the world.
Men 1,2	from everlasting to everlasting.
Men	thou art God
Woman 1	Thou turnest man back to the dust; and sayest, "Turn back, O children of men!"
Woman 2	For a thousand years in thy sight are but as yesterday when it is past.
Women 1,2	or as a watch in the night.
Men 1,2	Thou dost sweep men away;
Women 1,2	they are like a dream,
Women	like grass which is renewed in the morning:
Chorus	in the morning it flourishes, and is renewed,
Men	in the evening it fades and withers.
Chorus	For we are consumed in thine anger; by wrath we are overwhelmed.
Woman 1	Thou hast set our iniquities before thee,
Man 1	our secret sins in the light of thy countenance.
Woman 1	For all our days pass away under thy wrath.
Woman 1,2	our years come to an end like a sigh.
Woman 1,2	The days of our years are three-score and ten,
Women 1,2 Men 1,2	or even by reason of strength four-score;
Women	yet their span is but toil and trouble; they are soon gone and we fly away.
Men	Who considers the power of thy anger, and thy wrath according to the fear of thee?
Chorus	So teach us to number our days, that we may get a heart of wisdom.
Women 1,2	Return, O Lord how long?

*From the Revised Standard Version of the Bible. Copyrighted 1946, 1952. © 1971, 1972.

157

Women	Have pity on thy servants!
Women 1,2	Satisfy us in the morning with thy steadfast love,
Men	that we may rejoice and be glad all our days.
Woman 1	Make us glad as many days as thou hast afflicted us,
Woman 2	and as many as we have seen evil.
Man 1	Let thy work be manifest to thy servants,
Man 2	and thy glorious power to their children.
Women	Let the favor of the Lord our God be upon us:
Men	and establish thou the work of our hands upon us;
Chorus	yea, the work of our hands establish thou it.

Revised Standard Version

PSALM 118*

Note the swift change in mood and attitude.

Chorus	Give thanks to the Lord, for He is good;
	for His loving kindness is everlasting!/
Man	Let the house of Israel say,
Chorus	"For His loving kindness is everlasting."
Woman	Let those who worship the Lord say,
Chorus	"For His loving kindness is everlasting."
Solo	In my distress I cried out to my Lord,
	And He answered me with release.
Solo	The Lord is for me; I shall not fear.
	What can a man do to me?
Solo	The Lord is for me; He is my help.
	And I look in triumph on them that hate me.
	Chorus
Woman	It is better to rely on the Lord/than to put
	confidence in princes.
Solo	All nations encircled me and in the name of the Lord/
	Chorus
	I beat them down.

*From the Revised Standard Version of the Bible . Copyright 1946, 1952. © 1971, 1975.

	Chorus Solo
Solo	They encircled me,/*yes*/they were all about me but in
	Chorus
	the name of the Lord/I beat them down.
Solo	They swarmed around me as bees; they are burned out
	as a fire of thorns;
	Hard pressed, about to fall was I .
Chorus	but the Lord came to my help
A	The Lord is my strength and my song!
A B	He has become my salvation
A B C	The shout of joy and victory is in the tents of the
	righteous;
A D	the right hand of the Lord is doing valiantly.
C E	The right hand of the Lord is lifted up;
Chorus	The right hand of the Lord does valiantly.
Solo	I shall not die, but live, and tell of the
	Lord's deeds.
Solo	The Lord has chastened me sorely, but He has
	not given me over unto death.
Solo	Open to me the gates of righteousness;
	through them I will enter in and give thanks
	to the Lord.
Chorus	This is the gate of the Lord, and through it
	the righteous shall enter in.
Woman	I will give thanks to Thee for Thou has
	answered me and has become my deliverer.
Man	The stone which the builders rejected has
	become the head of the corner;
Solo	This is the Lord's doing, and it is marvelous
	in our eyes.
Chorus	This is the day which the Lord has made;
	Let us rejoice/and be glad in it.
Woman	O Lord, do grant salvation;
Man	Lord, do grant prosperity!
Chorus	Blessed is he who comes in the name of the
	Lord!

The chorus is divided into small groups A,B,C,D and E.

PSALM 147

(Man soloist speaks the added phrases)

Chorus	*Praise the Lord!* Solo *Why?*
	For it is good to sing praises to our God;
Solo 1	For he is gracious, and a song of praise is
	seemly. *Well, what does the Lord do?*
Solo 2	The Lord builds up Jerusalem; he gathers the
	outcasts of Israel.
Solo 3	He heals the brokenhearted, and binds up their
	wounds.
Solo 4	He determines the number of the stars, he gives
	to all of them their names.
Chorus	Great is our Lord/and abundant in power/
	his understanding is beyond measure/
Solo 5	The Lord lifts up the downtrodden, he casts the
	wicked to the ground.
Chorus	Sing to the Lord with thanksgiving;
Chorus	make melody to our God upon the lyre!
	How great is the power of God?
Solo 6	He covers the heavens with clouds, he prepares
	rain for the earth/he makes grass grow upon
	the hills.
	Solo 7
	He gives to the beasts their food, and to the
	young ravens which cry. *How may I please him?*
Solo 8	His delight is not in the strength of the
	horse, nor his pleasure in the legs of a man
Chorus	but the Lord takes pleasure in those who fear
	Him, in those who hope/in His steadfast love/

Revised Standard Version

vs.1-11

PSALM 150

(Use tambourine, drum, wood block or any rhythm instruments. Stress rhythm. Four beats to each line. You could also clap hands.)

Chorus	Praise the Lord (2 beats)
Chorus	Praise the Lord (2 beats)
Chorus	Praise the Lord / /
Woman	Praise / / /
Man	Praise / / /
Chorus	the Lord / / /
Woman	Praise / / /
Man	Praise / / /
Woman	Praise / / /
Man	Praise / / /
Chorus	the Lord / / /
Chorus	the Lord / / /
Woman	Praise / / /
Chorus	the Lord / / /
Man	Praise / / /
Chorus	the Lord / / /
Woman	Lord / / /
Man	Lord / / /
Chorus	Lord / / /
Woman	Praise / / /
Man	Praise / / /
Chorus	Lord / / /
Chorus	Praise the Lord / /
Chorus	Praise the Lord / /
Solo 1	Praise him with trumpet sound;
Solo 2	Praise him with lute and harp;
Solo 3	Praise him with tim—brel;
Solo 4	Praise him with strings and pipe;

(Use the instruments indicated if possible)

Add a voice	Let everything / / everything / / that breathes praise / / praise / / / the Lord / / /
Chorus	*Praise the Lord!* (no rhythm)

Adapted for use by the Northwestern College Choral Readers.

PSALM 151

By Peter Andringa

	I will return oh Lord to thy bosom/
Pauses	I will come again into thy temple/
should	I have seen women dancing in the streets/
be short	I have seen men dancing by the sea/
	I will be thine oh Lord to comfort
	I will return my soul to thee/
	I have sung praise to dancing women/
	I have played drums for marching men/
	I will not move from thee oh Lord
	I will be comforted by no other/
	I have turned from thee my God/
	I have seeking lost thee/
	I will return oh Lord to thy bosom/
	I will losing find thee./

Peter was a Northwestern College student and wrote this for the Northwestern College Choral Readers.

MODERN PSALMS*

These adapations of familiar Psalms speak to young people of the seventies. Intersperse the reading of the psalms with folk songs using guitars, bass fiddle, etc.

Narrator

The children of the inner city and their parents are often denied a chance to achieve goals. Many have little contact with anything successful; they seek to establish their own system of values and groupings, and even of religion. Status may depend on fights, flouting authority, and stealing. Beyond it all, there is still that cry for help and a desire to know God, but not according to the forms of a church that seemingly has already deserted them, holds out goals they cannot reach, and speaks words they do not understand.

These selections represent a search for a way in which spiritual truths can be taught in frames of reference that are real and vivid, in language and thought patterns that are understood, and that have meaning. It is an attempt to permit the so-called inner city adolescent to speak to us, rather than us to him.

Chorus

A GUY IS PRETTY SMART......Psalm 1
A guy is pretty smart
If he don't hang around with hoods
And do what they tell him.

He is smart too if he don't poke fun
At people who try to do the right thing.

He is always happy 'cause he knows for sure
That he is doing the right thing.

*From *God Is For Real, Man* by Carl F. Burke,©1966. Reprinted by permission of Association Press.

In fact it makes him feel so good
That he thinks about it day and night,
And that don't do no harm either.

He feel good 'cause this is God's way of doing things,
And you can't beat that.

This guy is sort of like a tree
In Humboldt Park
That grows by the lake.

It don't get looking like a droop
'Cause it gets plenty of water
And things to live from.

But the hoods are not like that—
They are like the dust that blows down the street
And all over the place,
And ya hate it.

So they won't stand a chance,
When the day comes to figure out the score
They will just get wiped up
And they won't be where the good guys are—

And that's for sure too.

That's 'cause God knows the way
People are
Down inside of them,
And you can't give him a snow job.

A hood may be on top now,
But it won't last.

GOD IS A GOOD HIDEOUT. . . . . .(Psalm 46)

God is a good hideout,
He is stronger than the weight lifter at the Y.
He helps you out even when you got trouble,
So what have you got to worry about even if there's a flood.
And the streets go caving in, and bridges get washed out?
When the creek is low it's easy to see how pretty it is
And that God is there.
But he is there when the creek's mad too.
When the going get rough, just remember that God is with us
Like he was with guys of old.

So take a look around—there's nice things—
As well as dirty empty lots and wrecked buildings.
Sometimes it's quiet-like at the end of the rumble.

So take time to think and you'll know about God—
And that he is here most of the time.

Solo   I WILL LOOK ABOVE THE HIGH RISERS   (Psalms 121)

I will look above the high risers.
        If I wants to find some help,
            It comes from God who made everything.

He won't let you get pushed around.
    He won't go to sleep on you
        And he will always be interested in you.
God is the kind of father
    That you wished you had.

No one can sneak up on you when he is around
    Either in the day or in the night
        Or when the street light's busted.

He will keep the big kids
    From beatin' on you,
        And they won't hurt you with him around.

God watches over you
   Every place you go
      And for all your life.

WE IS STILL FRIENDS, LORD*   (Psalm 86)

Put your ear next to me, Lord
I just want you to hear me and talk to me
'Cause I ain't got much.
Just remember I try to be like you.
You are my man
So I ask for your help.
Make me happy when I's mixed up inside.
We know you don't hold nothing against us
And you listen and hear us when we talk to you
And don't push me away.
So when we get troubles
We can call on you.

Help us remember you is only one
And everybody was made by you
And had sure better know it
And you are the only God.
Show me the right side of the street to walk on
So I can walk with you and even trust you
And not be afraid to say it
'Cause your love is just great.

When it seems like everybody is against me
And nothing goes right
And people is out to get me
Help me to know we is still friends
And that your love is here.
That's what helps me have heart.
So "Give me some skin," Lord,
Then everybody will know where we stand.

*Treat Me Cool Lord, by Carl F. Burke ©1968 reprinted by permission
of Association Press.

166

SELECTIONS FOR WORSHIP

The next group of numbers may be used for your worship services with young people or adults. Some are traditional, others carry a contemporary slant making them particularly usable today.

I suggest that your order "Fugue of Nations," a spoken rhythmic chant from Lexicon Music, Inc., and "Let's Just Praise the Lord" from Lyndale House Publishers, Wheaton, Illinois, 60187.

HEY, YOU!*
by James Caplan

Chorus   Hey, you!
You over there with the smile
    in your eyes, or the frown on
    your lips, or the tear on your
    cheek, or the song in your heart,
Who I don't even know your name yet.
Talk to me,
    Share with me,
    Be with me.
What is it that makes you you and me me?
What bothers you?
What excites you?
Is there anything more to you
    Than carbon, and bones, and skin?
What is it?
Do you love people?
Do you love God?
Do you act like you really are,
    or do you act like the people
    around you seem to want you to act?
I do, and I don't. Sometimes more,
    sometimes less.

*From *The Church Herald* January 31, 1969. Reprinted by permission of *The Church Herald.*

167

Hey you!
  Talk to me please.
Don't just talk about baseball.
Don't just tell me what's true.
There's a time for that but not now.
Why are you here tonight?
Why are you anywhere tonight—
  Is there some reason why
  you haven't committed suicide,
Gotten out of this world where
  people die and hearts break
  and all the fun and pleasure
  you can ever have can turn
  to dust in a minute?
You tell me your reason.
I'll tell you mine.

Solo: It started with a person who
  loved me, and said he would
  give me a satisfying, joyful life
If I would only want it.

Chorus: You tell me your reason.
I'll tell you mine.

(This is a good opening number).

LIFT AND DRAW

This may be used as a processional. Place a few readers on stage, then let the others come in from various seats in the auditorium, speaking as they take their places, then joining in with the group. Keep it moving fast with accurate rhythmical cues.

Stage group	This is a call to communicate the Word of God. But it is
	not easy to speak to our age. We are bombarded by words:
Solo 1	Black headlines in today's newspaper.
Solo 2	Shadowed images on a television screen.
Solo 3	Fast-paced patter from the car radio.

Solo 4	Color slashed in giant strokes on a billboard.
Solo 5	Buzzing-bright twists of neon lettering. A jangling phone and a crowed mailbox.
Stage group	We are called to communicate with every tool that God

solo 6

has given. Publicity is one way to reach a big and busy

solo 7   solo 8   solo 9   solo 10

world. Radio, television, newspaper, news networks that defeat the miles and conquer minutes:

Stage group	These can be part of God's way to shrink the world, to blind men into a reconciled community.

solo 12

Solo 11	Radio tubes and metal lines of type, newsmen dedicated to craft, truth, and significance:
Stage group	These can be God's tools to pierce men's disinterest and distraction,
Stage group	Ministers of the meaning. Christ belongs to the world. As stewards of the Living Word, we are called to be craftsmen of communication. To speak through the mass media by:
Solo 13	Building a program that shows Christ acting in our world today.
Solo 14	Telling our story with skill to inform, influence, interpret.
Solo 15	Understanding the newsman as someone to work with, not use.
Solo 16	Developing vision that sees the Good News beyond church news.
Solo 17	Giving thanks for the unfolding mystery of communication.
Chorus	Praying for the Living Word to move through our little words.

CHRISTIANS ALL

Chorus	Out of the past/the dim, dark ages,/came the voice of God. Asking/searching,/demanding an answer to his question;/ Where is thy brother?/ And the impudent man did not answer./He only said;/

Echo	Am I my brother's keeper?
Solo	Am I my brother's keeper? Add voices
	Am I my brother's keeper? Add voices
Chorus	Well, God didn't let the question go unanswered. /He spoke again. . ./and again./Through Moses he commanded:/
Solo	Thou shalt not kill.
Solo	Thou shalt not steal.
Solo	Thou shalt not commit adultery.
Solo	Thou shalt not bear false witness.
Solo	Thou shalt not covet thy neighbor's possessions.
Echo	Thou shalt love the Lord thy God with all thy
Chorus	heart and with all thy soul and with all thy strength and with all thy mind:/and thou shalt love thy neighbor as thyself./
Chorus	That was the word of God-/-the answer to the question/"Am I my brother's keeper?"/The answer was/"Yes." (Echo)
Chorus	But men forgot./Later the prophet Amos spoke for God, saying:/Woe to them that are at ease in Zion/. . .that lie upon beds of ivory and stretch themselves out upon their couches,/ and eat the lambs out of the flock and the calves out of the midst of the stall. ./.but they are not grieved for the affliction of Joseph./
Echo	Woe to them. ./.Woe to them./.Woe to them/
Chorus	And it came to pass that the people did not repent of their sins/but still mistreated their brethren, making slaves of many while loving idleness themselves./ And the Jews became captives in Babylon./. .And those who had lived in idleness became slaves/. . .Because they would not listen when God said:
Echo	Thou shalt love thy neighbor as thyself
Chorus	After fifty years in exile in Babylon, the Jews returned to Jerusalem and rebuilt the city./ Still they would not live together as brothers./
Solo	Some hated the Greeks. . .
Solo	Some hated the Romans. . .
Solo	Many hated the Samaritans. . .
Solo	The Pharisees hated the Sadducees. . .

Chorus	Then came Jesus. . ./ And he said;/
Solo	Ye have heard that it hath been said, "Thou shalt love thy neighbor and hate thine enemy." But I say unto you, Love your enemies, bless them that curse you, do good to them that hate you, and pray for them which despitefully use you and persecute you; that ye may be the children of your Father which is in heaven.
Chorus	Still people cried/
Echo Solo	Am I my brother's keeper?
Echo Solo	Who is my brother?
Echo Solo	Who is my neighbor?
Chorus	Jesus answered not only with words but with his life./As he went about Galilee, healing the sick and comforting the lonely,/people saw that his neighbors were the men and women, boys and girls of many towns./They saw that his neighbors were the rich and the poor,/the clever and the crude,/the dark and the light,/the Jew and the Gentile./ They saw that Jesus was his brother's keeper./Nearly two thousand years have come and gone since Jesus came to speak for God/and to live as God among us./Still people ask:/
Echo	Am I my brother's keeper?/Who is my brother?/
Chorus	And Jesus tells us again:
Solo	Then shall the king say to them on his right hand, Come O blessed of my Father, inherit the kingdom prepared for you from the foundation of the world:
Echo solo	For I was hungry and you gave me food,
Echo Solo	I was thirsty and you gave me drink,
Echo solo	I was a stranger and you welcomed me,
Echo solo	I was naked and you clothed me,
Echo solo	I was sick and you visited me,
Echo solo	I was in prison and you came to me.
Chorus	Then the righteous will answer him:/
Chorus	Lord, when did we see thee hungry and feed thee,/or thirsty and give thee drink?/And when did we see thee sick or in prison and visit

171

	thee?/And the King will answer them:/
Solo	Truly, I say to you, as you did it to one of the least of these thy brethren, you did it to me. Remember, then:
Chorus	When the hungry children of the world are fed through gifts of money or goods, Christ is fed,/when missionaries go for us to satisfy the thirst of people for the good news of God's love, the Master of Men is refreshed,/When the homeless crowds of migrant workers are given good places to use for houses,/Christ enters the door with them./
Chorus	When we share our money or clothes to warm someone who is poorly clothed,/the Son of God is warmed./When we help to send doctors or nurses to heal the sick and protect the young and old alike from disease and accident,/we send servants of Jesus,/When we forgive those who do us wrong and help them to share in a friendly world,/God's will is done./ Ask no more, then,/ "Who is my brother?" He is:
Echo solo	Your next door neighbor. . .
Echo solo	The man who collects the rubbish. . .
Echo solo	A boy picking oranges when he should be in school. . . .
Echo solo	The Sailor helping to bring your food from a distant island. . .
Echo Solo	And a Chinese boy named Chan who has never heard of Jesus Christ.
Chorus	Ask no more,/Am I my brother's keeper?"/Bear ye one another's burdens, and so fulfill the law of Christ. In this way you can make the Spirit of Christ a living power.
Solo	You can make yours a better town. . .
Solo	And a better nation. . .
Solo	And a better world.
Chorus and Echo	*You can be your brother's brother!*

Place a group of readers at the back of the room to serve as an echo chorus.

A LITANY OF THE LORD'S PRAYER

Chorus
: When friendly words grow faint and friendly hands are few, and life becomes a desert waste,/ teach us still to pray/

Solo
: OUR FATHER, WHO ART IN HEAVEN.

Chorus
: When irreverence invades the sanctities of the soul. And profane words strike home upon our ears/teach us still to pray/

Solo
: HALLOWED BE THY NAME.

Chorus
: When darkness broods over the deep and sin mounts the throne of power/Teach us still to pray,/

Solo
: THY KINGDOM COME
When leaders of men impose their will upon the ways of earth/Teach us still to pray,/

Solo
: THY WILL BE DONE ON EARTH AS IT IS IN HEAVEN

Chorus
: When anxious thought of coming days disturbs our inward calm./Teach us still to pray/

Solo
: GIVE US THIS DAY OUR DAILY BREAD.

Chorus
: When grieved by our many sins and hurt by the sins of others,/Teach us still to pray,/

Solo
: FORGIVE US OUR DEBTS AS WE FORGIVE OUR DEBTORS. When desires burn like a consuming fire/and purity loses its lure,/Teach us still to pray,/

Solo
: AND LEAD US NOT INTO TEMPTATION. BUT DELIVER US FROM EVIL

Chorus
: When the task of the day is done/and we sink in night's repose,/Teach us still to pray,/

Chorus
: FOR THINE IS THE KINGDOM, AND THE POWER, AND THE GLORY FOREVER, AMEN.

Chorus	A certain man entered the sanctuary of his church one day./He had been blessed with things and goods and loved ones, and he wanted to pray./He folded his hands./. .he bowed his head./ . .and prayed./Our Father, who art in heaven. . ./
Solo	Wait a minute! Whose Father did you say he was? Did you say, "Our Father?" Would you include the Negro, the Jew, the Japanese, in that "Our Father?". . .Is he the Father of the convict, the enemy?. . .Do you really want to say "Our Father?"
Chorus	Our Father, who art in heaven, hallowed by thy name. . .
Solo	Did you say "Hallowed be thy name?". . .Keep the name of God holy. . .You have not cursed me with ill words. . .but you have removed holiness and reverence from my name by using it glibly. . .without obligation, without responsibility. . .You bear God's name as men call you Christian. Do you mean to say that in your life God's name is kept holy? You have grown in favor with man, but have you grown in favor with God?
Chorus	Thy kingdom come. . .
Solo	Whose kingdom?. . .You don't want God's kingdom. . .it will mean the giving up of this world's goods for others—it will mean sacrifice, easing beds of pain, nursing the sick, binding the broken-hearted, befriending the lonely, bearing the cross. . .the cross of others. . .God's kingdom isn't a bed of roses. To obtain it you walk a road that becomes a path. . .where men walk singly and alone. . .toward a hill, a hill called Calvary. . .and they die for what they believe to be right.
Chorus	Thy will be done on earth as it is in heaven. . .
Solo	God's will be done in your life? Will you who let so many people run your life, let God have his

way with your life? Can God go with you where you go? Can you go where God leads? Are you willing to take God to the places where you go? God wills mercy, justice, truth! Heaven is beauty, and hope, and love. Do you really want heaven on earth for everyone?

Chorus	Give us this day our daily bread...
Solo	Us?...Our daily bread?...There are countless millions of refugees, men, women, and children existing on what you toss away as refuse... LISTEN!...Do you hear that child crying? She's crying for bread. "Us"..."Our"...Have you given up anything in your young life to help provide them with bread? In the face of such starvation, I ask you...you who pray for "Our Daily Bread." Are you still eating the same food in the same complaining way as you used to?...Are you wasteful of bread? You can do something about helping God provide daily bread for all his children...Do you know what it feels to pass up a meal and not be able to do anything about it? How would you feel if your sister cried meal after meal for food and it could not be provided? What if she were your sister, slowly starving...white...ribs exposed ... gaunt, haggard, dirty, dying...for want of bread....
Chorus	And forgive us our debts as we forgive our debtors...
Solo	No...don't say that...you can't mean it. Are you reciting or praying? Do you want your debts forgiven in the way you forgive the debts of others? You have not forgiven...You have not even forgotten...You remember old quarrels and old wars. You recall old gossip and relish the latest scandal about your neighbors. You don't want that kind of forgiveness meted out to you...You don't want God to forgive....
Chorus	And lead us not into temptation....
Solo	God does not lead you into temptation too

175

	strong for you. But he is always available and sufficient power against evil. But have you always availed yourself of this power? Do you seek him in all people and all places? Have you stored up spiritual resources for days of spiritual famine?
Chorus	But deliver us from evil...
Solo	You who like to live so near the brink of the precipice of evil...Do you want to be delivered from evil?...You have courted it so long and ardently? You have forgotten your Savior's admonition to "taste, and see how good the Lord is."...You have tasted everything else...so much so that you have lost the taste of the good and the beautiful and the holy.
Chorus	For Thine is the Kingdom, and the Power...
Solo	Have you not tried to build you own kingdom? ...Kingdoms and powers are of God...And they come to those who want them enough...want them so earnestly that they will suffer to get them...A sincere prayer will bring a triumphant answer from a holy God.
Chorus	For Thine is the Kingdom, and the power, and the Glory/forever./AMEN./

This selection needs a strong soloist.

A LITANY FOR RACIAL JUSTICE

Chorus	O Lord, Father and protector of us all/Thou who made us brothers and joined all hands with the common link of love:/
Solo	Search us, O God, and know our hearts; try us and know our thoughts.
Chorus	Father, we have strayed from thy precepts/We have sinned against our brothers/
Solo	By withdrawal from their presence,
Solo	By ignorance and neglect of their human needs

176

Solo	By absence of warmth and friendship,
Solo	By silence in the midst of wrong,
Solo	By empty promises too long postponed.
Chorus	If we say we have no sin,/we deceive ourselves. We are not guiltless of the insult of separation and the crime of injustice./Upon our Pilate-hands are the tears and the blood of our brother's desperation./On our consciences is the despair of the deprived/
Solo	The thirsty who cannot drink,
Solo	The hungry who cannot eat,
Solo	The weary who cannot rest,
Solo	The disfranchised confined outside the gates of opportunity,
Solo	The shackled, the crippled, the disenchanted, the
Chorus	slain Wilt thou not revive us again?/Show us thy mercy, O Lord, and grant us thy salvation/Help us tear down the barriers that divide us from our neighbors:/Clear out cluttered gardens with the sunlight of thy love/Uproot the stubborn weeds of intolerance and bigotry from the sandy clay of indifference./Cover the ground with the fertile soil of goodwill/. And plant the seeds of unity and justice there./Fortify us/commit us to thy righteousness.

A MODERN PARABLE

Solo	In the beginning there was a man, a rational, thinking, laughing, featherless, sex-driven, passionate creature, who decided he was lonely.

                              men   solo

And man said: "Let there be light." And there was

               Chorus

light, fluorescent bulbs and incadescent bulbs, neon signs and luminescent panelling, sun lamps and mercury vapor lamps, General Electric and

              solo

Westinghouse all blinking on and off. And Man used this light to eliminate the darkness. And the

177

day was night and the night was day. And all was
chorus solo
light. (At the touch of a switch) And man saw the
solo
light and said he could see.

Solo

And man made Connecticut power and light to
rule New England, and Con Edison to rule New
York. And to each state he assigned its appropriate
Chorus
light. And the rest of the world burned matches.
solo
And man divided East from West.

Solo

men
And man said: "Let there be heaven and earth."
And man used fertilizers and chemicals to increase
medium women join in
the output of his farms, he used dredges to reclaim
the swamps and urban renewal projects to rebuild
dark women join in
the cities. He used barometers and thermometers
and cloud seeding devices to predict and control
Chorus
the weather. And he sent rockets into *space* to
follow the paths of the telescopes—to circle the
sun.

Solo
Solo

And man saw the earth and longed for the heavens.
men chorus
Then man said: "Let there be life." And he
dissected frogs and injected rats with hypodermic
needles and locked mice in skinner boxes. He saw
the amoeba and protozoa and broke into the living
cell. He analyzed guinea pigs and even analyzed
himself. He invented the world of "Id" and
inhabited it with Egos, with psychoses, Oedipus
complexes, sibling rivalries, and paranoic
schizophrenia. men

Solo

And man said: "Here is life."

Solo

men Solo
And then man said: "Let there be God." But he

couldn't decide what type of god he should have,

                                      solo 2   solo 3
so he first made him (a cat's head), (or a horse's
                  solo 4   solo
body), (or in the shape of the sun). But these

didn't satisfy man, and so he made God in his own

image. He gave him a long white beard and told
                     chorus
him he was infinte, omniscient, omnipresent,

                                            solo
perfect, incomprehensible, and on my side. He told

him that he was so much on my side that he died
for me.

Chorus   And man made God and set him on a pedestal and
went back to his work and blew himself up.

Solo   AND IN THE END THERE WAS GOD!

Use your imagination, plenty of rhythm and
sparkle, to make this number effective. The
audience will be surprised and moved by the
bomb-shell ending. Choose your soloist carefully.
The timing is very important.

RECEPTION GOOD*

Narrator	Now, at a particular spot on the radio dial,
Solo 1	"—In this corner, wearing purple trunks—"
Narrator	Mingles, somehow, with the news that—
Solo 2	"Powerful enemy units have been surrounded in the drive,"
Narrator	And both of these with the information that—
Solo 3	"There is a way to avoid having chapped and roughened hands."
Narrator	Such are the new and complex harmonies it seems of a strange and still more complex age.

*Reprinted by permission. Estate of Kenneth Fearing. Mattison and
Koenig.

	It is not that the reception is confused or poor, but rather
	it is altogether too clear and good. And no worse, in any case, than that other receiving set, the mind, forever faithfully transmitting the great and little impulses that arrive, however wavering or loud, from near and far.
Solo 4	"It is an ill wind—"
Narrator	It is apt to report, underscoring this with
Solo 5	"—The bigger they are the harder they fall,"
Narrator	And simultaneously reminding, darkly, that
Solo 6	"Thing are seldom as they seem."
Narrator	Reconciling, with ease the irreconcilable, Piecing together fragments of a flashing past with clouded snapshots of the present and future, Fashioning a raw, wild symphony of a wedding march, a drinking song, and a dirge, Multiplying enormous figures with precision, then raising the question:
Solo 7	"But after all, what is a man?"
Narrator	Somehow creating hope and fresh courage out of ancient doubt.
Solo 8	"Both boys are on their feet, they're going to it."
Narrator	The radio reports,
Solo 9	"—The sinking was attended by a heavy loss of life—"
Solo 10	"—This amazing cream for quick, miraculous results."
Chorus	How many pieces are there in a simple jigsaw puzzle?/ How many phases of a man's life can crowd their way into a single moment?/How many angels,/actually,/can dance on the point of a pin?/

by Kenneth Fearing

Reception Good illustrates the importance of communication and the danger to society when there is a breakdown. Use several soloists with voice suited to the lines. A narrator unites it all.

HELLO

Solo	Did you call, Christ? You did?
l w	From where are you calling me?
l m	From the council above?
d w	The mountain?
d m	The Father's house?
Chorus	The word.
Solo	It doesn't matter where?
Chorus	No, it doesn't
	I suppose
Solo	But it's hard to hear you.
	Sometimes.
l w	Very hard.
l m	You speak with us
d w	As God would speak.
d m	You are the word of God.
Chorus	You say/
Chorus	Okay.
Chorus	And now you ask us all to speak./
	To go and talk to God/
	To talk it up.
	To live it up.
	And change our world./
Solo	Seems simple.
	So simple.
Chorus	But it's not./
	It's rough.
l w	Like skiing
l m	Or forgiving.
d w	Could you help us
d m	Perhaps?/
Solo	Could you?
Chorus	Yes, we'll try./
	But—
	We're busy too!/
Chorus	Well help us to talk
l w	To say the words.
l m	To live the talk.
d w	And make our speech
d m	A song,

Chorus	A sacrament.
Solo	A strange word?
	But you know what we mean.
	Our God alive
	Within our words.
	Right?
Chorus	What should we talk about?
Solo	Specifically?
Solo	All things.
Solo	How about you yourself
d w	And pimples and God
l m	And quivering lips and you.
d w	And eggs and hidden embryos
d m	And fresh blood and you.
w	And dirty dollars and hair curlers
m	And guinea pigs and you
Chorus	And us
d w m	And genes
l w m	And grace
Solo	And you?
Chorus	But how?
	How much at a time?
	And when?
Solo	That's not secondary
	At all!
Chorus	Then
	Form the word "Forgive"
	Upon our lips
	And between our teeth/.
l w	Unite our tongues.
l m	Untangle our minds
d w	To see and say.
d m	"I will forgive.
Chorus	For God forgives
Chorus	Others just like me."
	To say it
	And mean it
	And live it/
	But that's hard
	So hard to do.
Solo	Someone is coming, Lord.

But don't go.
What shall I say?
l w   "Hi."
d w   "Nice day."

WHO WILL CAST THE FIRST STONE?

Solo
woman   ...The woman lies before Christ in a huddled
heap, sobbing as she listens to the indictment.
The penalty for adultery is stoning. Jesus' steady
eyes take in the situation at a glance. He sees
what they try to hide from him—the hard faces
that have no mercy or pity. Every hand holds a
stone and clutching fingers along the sharp edges
with malicious satisfaction.

They have brought the woman to Christ as a
vindictive afterthought, not for formal trial, (for
they have already tried her) but as a bold effort
to trap him.

Either He will have to set aside the plain
commandment of the law, or tacitly consent to
a public execution. . . .And has He not said
often, "Be ye therefore merciful?" How can He
condemn the woman and still be merciful? The
circle of bearded men waits impatiently for His
answer. . . .

Christ looks into the faces of the men before
Him, and steadily—with eyes that never blink—
He speaks to them: "He that is without sin
among you, Let him cast a stone at her." His
keen glance rests upon the woman's accusers one
by one. . . .There is the thud of stone after stone
falling on the pavement. Not many of the
Pharisees are left now. Looking into their faces,
Christ sees into the yesterdays that lie deep in
the pools of memory and conscience. He sees
into their very hearts. . . .

Solo man	Idolator. . . .
Solo man	Liar. . .
Solo man	Drunkard. . . .
Solo man	Murderer. . .
Solo man	Adulterer. . .
Solo (women)	One by one they creep away—like animals—slinking into the shadows. . . . .Shuffling off into the crowded streets to lose themselves in the multitudes.
Chorus	"He that is without sin among you, let him cast the first stone at her."

GOD MUST KNOW AN AWFUL LOT

I suggest using slide projections with this contemporary number. The soloist should be a boy. This offers good solo training for a number of readers.

Solo	God, last night I looked at the stars, And I saw
Light Woman	Andromeda
Dark Woman	Orion
Light Woman	Jupiter
Dark Woman	Luna
Chorus	Like a mobile of suspended orbs.
Solo	I saw the
Chorus	cosmos of your creation.
Solo	God, you must know an awful lot about physics.
Solo	Yesterday I read about

Light Man	DNA
Light Woman	Cytoplasm
Dark Woman	Neurons.
Solo	I studied
Light Woman	Respiration
Light Woman	Replication
Dark Woman	Photosynthesis
Solo	Through a microscope I saw
Light Man	Amoebae
Light Woman	Paramecia
Dark Man	Algae
Chorus	I saw life.
Solo	God, you must know
	an awful lot about biology.
Solo	Yesterday I played
Dark Man	Football
Dark Man	Baseball
Light Man	Soccer,
Solo	And I
Light Man	Swam
Light Woman	Ran
Dark Man	Swung
Dark Woman	Climbed,
Solo	And I watched my feet
	And legs and arms and hands.
	I saw the incredible
	engineering behind them. (with gesture)
Men	I felt their impossible dexterity.
	God, you must know
	an awful lot about athletics.
Solo	Yesterday I saw
	a picture of a brain
Women	That cellular mass
	that allowed me
Light Woman	to reason
Dark Woman	and decide
Light Woman	and love
Dark Woman	and hate
Chorus	all on my own.
Solo	Then I looked at boxes
	filled with tapes,

light woman   dark woman
circuits and memory banks,
chorus

Solo	And saw/what a pitiful facsmilie they are next to that mass of cells.
Men	And I thought.
Solo	God, you must know an awful lot about psychology.
Solo	Yesterday I heard the voices you gave to
Light man	Caruso
Light Woman	Munsel
Dark Woman	Callas
Solo	I realized the talent you gave
Dark Woman	Gershwin
Dark Man	Bach
Light Man	Tchaikovsky.

light man   dark man
I heard Sinatra and Campbell

Solo	God, you must know an awful lot about music.
Solo	Yesterday I read about
Light Man	Socrates
Dark Man	Descartes
Dark Man	Kierkegaard.
Solo	And I watched people—
Chorus	All kinds of people.
Solo	I saw them searching
Chorus	for meaning.
Solo	Then I knew you had given everyone
Chorus	spiritual need.
Solo	God, you must know an awful lot about philosophy.
Solo	Today I read about Jesus. I read that he's
Chorus	your only Son—
Men	An extension of yourself.
Solo	I read about his life,

186

Man	And about his Death;
	Chorus
Woman	How you sent him/to
	Take the rap for me;
Woman	How you deserted him
Chorus	—for me.
Chorus	How he was
Light Woman	Scorned
Women	Spat on
Women	
Light Men	Mocked
Chorus	Beaten
	Tortured
	for me.
	For worthless me.
	And all this because
Light Woman	You
Dark Woman	Really
Women	Cared for me.
Solo	God, you must know
	an awful lot about love.
	I can't help wondering,
	God.
Chorus	Why do people ignore you?

by Tim Nelson

WHY?

Chorus	I walked today through the slums of life—down the dark streets of wretchedness and of pain. I trod today where few have trod and as I walked, I questioned God.
Solo 1	I saw the prostitutes in the dance halls.
Solo 2	I saw the sots in the bar room.
Solo 3	I saw the thieves as they picked pockets.
Chorus	I saw men and women devoid of life—living in world of sin—and above the din I whispered, "Why, God, why?"

187

Chorus	I walked today down the lanes of hate, hearing the jeers of bitter men, hearing the names they cursed and spat—
	solo 5 solo 6 solo 7
Solo 4	"dago" "nigger," "kike," "jap."
Chorus	I saw the dejected men they stoned. I felt the anguish of their cries. I saw them as they slapped the lonely, as they turned their backs on human needs. Snarling, growling were the fiends of hell. These God called His sons!
Solo	Gasping for air I cried:
Chorus	"Why, God why?"
Solo	I walked today through war's grim dread—over the fields of blood, over graveless men. I saw the dead, the crucified, the headless, the limbless, the pleading, the crying. I saw the pain, the waste; I smelled the odor of rotted flesh. I saw the children gathered 'round—watching naked, hungry, weeping, diseased, dirty—the baby trying to nurse from a dead mother. The ruins—the agony—the despair! Disaster all around! Blinded with tears, I fled down the streets. I stumbled, then stopped. I shouted, "Why, God? Why do you let men sin, suffer, hate? Unmerciful Father? God, art Thou blind— art Thou wicked and cruel? God, how canst Thou watch and do naught? Why must this be?" (Chorus gathers close to soloist)

The world grew silent. I awaited reply. The silence was heavy. I started to tremble. I waited long—half rebuking, half fearing. Then I heard from close behind me (chorus softly) "Why, Man? Why?"

PRAYER OF ST. FRANCIS OF ASSISI

Following are two benedictions or closing numbers. *The Prayer of St. Francis Assisi* is effective accompanied by a worship choir. The robed choir pantomimes the implied action as the speaking choir reads. Sticks may be used here also.

Lord make me an instrument of your peace:
Where there is hatred let me bring love;
Where there is injury pardon;
Where there is doubt faith;
Where there is despair hope;
Where there is darkness light;
Where there is sadness joy.
O divine Master grant that I may not so
much seek to be consoled as to console;
To be understood as to understand;
To be loved as to love.
For it is in giving that we receive;
It is in pardoning that we are pardoned;
And it is in dying that we are born to
eternal life.

DOXOLOGY

Chorus

We praise thee, our God, Father,
Son and Holy Spirit;
Who didst find us in estrangement;/
Who didst heal our rebellious hearts;/
Who didst prepare us for life eternal with thee./
To thee be all praise, honor, glory, dominion
    and power,
In this world and the next./
Hallelujah!

(Could be chanted)

BENEDICTION

Eleanor Powers

The sun be warm and kind
To you,
The darkest night some star
Shine through,
The dullest morn
A radiance brew,
And when dusk comes—
God's hand
To you.

AN OLD GAELIC RUNE

Deep peace of the running wave to you,
Deep peace of the flowing air to you,
Deep peace of the quiet earth to you,
Deep peace of the shining stars to you,
Deep peace of the watching shepherds to you,
Deep peace of the Son of Peace to you.

FEATURE NUMBERS FOR SACRED PROGRAMS

These are longer selections and may be used during a worship service as a sermon or message.

Vernon Hoff's selection *For This He Came* has been performed hundreds of times by the Northwestern College Choral Readers. It is a moving never to be forgotten experience in living the beautiful story of Jesus.

FOR THIS HE CAME*
by
Vernon L. Hoffs

For This He Came was written by Rev. Hoffs, a minister and missionary in the Reformed Church, for his young people in a Denver church. It takes twenty minutes to produce and is an excellent feature number for a worship service. Let the soloists move freely as they speak, and the chorus should rise, or even stand on their benches for the climactic sequences. The soloists are three boys, three girls, a man and a woman.

FOR THIS HE CAME

Chorus	This is a true story. The story of a Savior. Your Savior, my Savior, Savior of all the world. The Savior of this church. (chorus is seated)
Girl 1	Listen well!
Girl 2	You are a part of this story. It could change your life.
Boy 1	Where do we begin?
Chorus	Where else but in the beginning.
Man	In the beginning. . .God!
Woman	In the beginning God created the Heavens and the earth, the sea and all that in them is.
Man	On the sixth day the Lord God created a creature unlike all the rest.

*Reprinted by permission of Rev. Vernon L. Hoffs.

Woman	This creature was. . .man!
Boy 2	But how created?
Man	God created man in his own image, in the image of God created He them, male and female created He them.
Girl 3	And he lived where?
Woman	God planted a garden eastward in Eden. Here they lived. Adam and his wife Eve. God told them to be fruitful and multiply and replenish the earth.
Chorus	But they sinned! Adam and Eve sinned against the Almighty God!
Man	Sinned! Impossible! Man was created in the image of God, how could he sin?
Chorus	Adam and Eve disobeyed God!
Boy 3	What had God told them?
Woman	God had said "You may freely eat of every tree of the garden. But of the tree of knowledge of good and evil you shall not eat, for in the day that you eat of it, you shall die!"
Chorus	They would die!
Girl 3	If they ate they would die!
Boy 3	This was God's command!
Boy 2	But the devil said to them. . .
Woman	You will not die, for God knows that in the day you eat thereof you will become as God, knowing good and evil.
Boy	The devil lied!
Girl 2	He told them nothing but lies!
Man	What did they do?
Woman	They ate the fruit.
Chorus	They sinned! They sinned! They must die! The wages of sin is death. This is God's command!
Chorus	God is just, but they must die! To sin is to die!
Woman	This is how sin first began. Because Adam and Eve sinned, you and I are now sinful and are under the curse of the law.

Man	What a fool man is, don't you think? He deserves to die. What did he ever do for God! If I were God I would strike him to the dust from whence he came.
Woman	NO! God will not forsake them all. God is love. God will save them. God is just, but God is also love!
Chorus	Save them God! Save them!
Man	How can He save them? Man could never take the punishment of God. Man is too weak, too feeble. Man is human!
Boy 1	...This is where the real story begins.
Girl 1	The story of the Savior, Jesus Christ the Son of God!
Woman	For God so loved the world that He gave His only begotten Son that whosoever believeth on Him should not perish but have everlasting life.
Chorus	How great the love of God! How great the love of Christ to die for our sins.
Man	This is why Jesus Christ came to earth.
Woman	Jesus came to earth to seek and to save those who are lost.
Chorus	We are the youth of his church. He came to save us.
Girl 2	To save you, our parents.
Girl 2	To save you, our friends.
Boy 1	To save you, the church.
Man	So begins the story...
Woman	Where was he born?
Boy 1	In Judea
Boy 3	Of the house of David
Man	Caesar Augustus had sent out an official decree that everyone was to go to his own city to be counted in the great census. So Mary and Joseph, the earthly parents of Jesus went to Bethlehem because they were of the family of King David.
Woman	While they were there the days were accomplished that she should be delivered and Mary gave birth to the Son of God.

193

Chorus	Jesus Christ. . .The Son of God. . .Born a babe in Bethlehem. How humble. How great. He was born in a stable for you, for me, and for this church.
Girl 2	Behold the King of Heaven is here!
Girl 3	The long wait is over.
Boy 1	The Messiah has come at last
Chorus	For you. . .For me. . .For all sinful men He has come.
Woman	And when the days of Mary's purification, according to the law of Moses, were accomplished they brought Him to Jerusalem to present Him to the Lord. The High Priest Simeon took the babe in his arms and said. . .
Man	Behold, this child is set for the rising and falling of many!
Chorus	And the child grew and waxed strong in spirit, filled with wisdom and the grace of God was upon Him.
Girl	And Jesus increased in wisdom, and stature,
Boy 3	And in favor with God and man.
Chorus	Blessed be the name of God and Christ His Son. . .our Redeemer.
Man	And after thirty years Jesus began to go out through all the land preaching, healing, and warning the people to repent and believe on the words of God.
Woman	The Kingdom of God was at hand. . .The Kingdom of God is at hand. Believe on the Lord Jesus Christ and thou shall be saved.
Boy 2	This is why He came.
Girl 1	To save you and to save me.
Boy 1	To save this church from death.
Chorus	Blessed are all that hear these words and believe.
Woman	And Jesus called unto Himself twelve men. . . Apostles the building stones of the church. . . this church. Their names were. . .
Boy 1	Peter. . .James. . .Andrew. . .
Boy 2	and John
Girl 1	Philip, Bartholomew, and Matthew the Publican.

Girl 2	Thomas the Doubter, and James. . .
Boy 3	Thaddeus, Simon. . .
Girl 3	And last of all, Judas the Traitor,
Chorus	Judas the Traitor. . .Sinful, wicked Judas. . . He betrayed the Christ. (climax—chorus up)
Girl 1	Are you betraying the Christ? (chorus sits)
Girl 2	Repent and believe, for the Kingdom of God. . .
Boy 1	. . .was at hand
Boy 2	. . .is at hand.
Man	The disciples came to Jesus and said to Him.
Woman	Lord, teach us to pray.
Man	And Jesus said to them, After this manner therefore pray ye.

Song: "The Lord's Prayer" (may be sung here
while chorus remains seated with bowed
heads)

Man	For about three years Jesus went about Galilee, Judea and Samaria preaching and teaching the words of God.
Girl 1	But they wouldn't listen. . .
Boy 1	They despised Him. . .
Woman	Fools! What fools they are! Don't they know He was sent by God?
Girl 2	Why won't they listen?
Girl 1	He is God. . .He is your King our Saviour
Boy 1	Why won't they listen?
Chorus	Why? Why? (chorus stands)
Woman	And it came to pass after three years the chief priests and scribes met continually, plotting and planning how they might kill Him.
Girl 2	But why do they want to destroy him?
Boy 2	Because He was God and His words and accusations offended them.
Girl 3	What fools. . .
Girl 2	To kill their Saviour. . .
Chorus	Foolish men! Foolish unto death! (chorus sits)
Man	Now the feast of the unleavened bread drew nigh, which is called the Passover.

Woman	Then entered Satan into Judas the Traitor, who was one of the twelve.
Chorus	Evil Judas! He betrayed his Savior!
Boy 3	Whad did Judas do?
Girl 1	He went to the chief priests and they gave him. .
Boy 1	Money. . .
Girl 2	Thirty pieces of silver they gave him for Christ.
Boy 2	The price of a slave.
Chorus	He sold his Savior for the price of a slave!
Woman	Then came the day of the unleavened bread when the lamb must be killed. . .
Man	And when the hour was come, Christ sat down in the Upper Room with His disciples and they ate the. . .
Chorus	Passover!
Woman	And as they sat, Jesus took bread and gave thanks, and break it saying. . .
Chorus	This is my body which is given for you, this do in remembrance of me.
Man	Likewise also He took the cup, gave thanks, and gave to them saying. . .
Chorus	This is the blood of the New Testament which is shed for many, for the remission of sins.
Woman	Thus they had eaten
Chorus	The Last Supper.
Man	Having finished the meal, Jesus and His disciples went out to the Mount of Olives and going a little farther He fell to His knees and began to pray saying. . .
Woman	. . .Father, if Thou be willing, remove this cup from me, nevertheless not my will, but Thine be done.
Girl 3	Cup?. . .what does He mean. . .cup?
Boy 3	He must die. . .
Girl 2	For men He must die. . .
Chorus	Look at Him. . .how humble. . .how sinless . . .how perfect. . .and yet. . .
Girl 1	He must die. . .
Boy 1	. . .for you
Girl 2	. . .for me. . .
Chorus	. . .for this church.

Woman	And behold while He spake there came a multitude with swords and torches and also Judas.
Boy 1	. . .swords?. . .for the Son of God?
Boy 2	. . .how foolish!
Man	And after Judas the traitor had betrayed his Savior with a kiss, the multitude immediately laid hold on Jesus and led Him away to be tried before the governor. . . Pontius Pilate.
Girl 1	. . .And His disciples. . .what happened to them?
Girl 2	They fled! they were scared. . .they fled.
Girl 3	And Judas?
Boy 2	He went and hanged himself
Woman	Thus they took Jesus and set Him before Pilate, and Pilate asked Him saying. . .
Man	Art Thou the King of the Jews?
Girl 3	And Jesus answered. . .
Boy 3	Thou sayest it.
Chorus	And the multitudes accused Jesus of many things.
Woman	Now it was custom at the feast that the governor should release unto the multitude one prisoner, and there was besides Jesus one man who was guilty of murder. . .his name was Barabbas!
Girl 2	And Pilate said to the crowds. . .
Man	Whom will ye that I release unto you? Barabbas or Jesus which is called the Christ?
Woman	And then they cried with one voice. . .
Chorus	Barabbas!. . .Barabbas!. . .Give us Barabbas! Away with Jesus! we want Barabbas! We want Barabbas! Give us Barabbas! (climax: chorus up)
Woman	And Pilate answered them saying. . .
Man	What then shall I do with Him who is called Christ, the King of the Jews?
Woman	And they shouted in a loud voice. . .
Chorus	. . .Crucify! Crucify Him! Let Him be Crucified! Crucify Him! (add voices until full choir is reached—climax)

197

Woman	Pilate then arose, took water and washed his hands before the people and cried. . .
Man	Take Him then and crucify Him, but I am innocent of the blood of this Man. See ye to it!
Woman	And they led Jesus away. . .
Chorus	And crucified Him!
Girl 3	On Golgotha. . .
Girl 2	The place of the skull. . .here they hung Him on a Cross. . .
Girl 1	. . .and drove nails into His hands and feet
Chorus	On a cross He suffered. . .
Boy 3	For you. . .
Girl 2	For this church
Chorus	On a cross He died. . .
Boy 3	For you
Girl 1	For me
Girl 2	For this church (chorus sits)
Woman	Have we finished the story?
Chorus	NO!! the best is yet to come! Behold, the Victory is near! Watch!. . .Listen. . .We will tell you of the Victory!
Boy	My victory. . .
Girl 1	Your victory
Boy 2	Christ's victory
Chorus	The victory of this church. . .
Man	Lo, there came a rich man from Arimathea whose name was Joseph. He came and took the body of Jesus, wrapped it in a linen cloth and laid it in a tomb.
Woman	And he sealed the tomb with a. . .
Chorus	Rock!
Woman	After three days had passed, three women. . .
Girl 2	Mary the mother of James. . .
Chorus	. . .Salome. . .
Boy 3	and Mary Magdalene. . .
Woman	. . .came to the tomb to anoint the body of Jesus with spices.
Man	As they drew near unto the tomb, behold!. . .
Girl 1	. . .the rock was gone. . .
Boy 2	. . .the tomb was open. . .

Girl 1	the rock had been removed.
Woman	As they entered the tomb they saw an angel who said unto them, He is not here. He has. . .(Chorus up)
Chorus	Risen! Hallelujah. . .Christ is risen. He has broken the bonds of death! Hallelujah, Hallelujah! (Song: "Hallelujah Chorus" played on organ) Climax
Man	Forty days after He had risen from the tomb, Christ appeared unto His disciples and He said unto them. . .
Woman	Lo, I am with you always, even unto the end of time.
Man	And while the disciples were watching, He was
Girl 1	. . .taken up into heaven
Boy 1	. . .Taken up on a cloud. . .
Boy 2	. . .and received out of their sight.
Chorus	He returned to the Father to come again at the end of time.
Woman	Is the story finished?
Chorus	No, this story will never end. It will continue for ever and ever. This is our Christ. . .
Girl 2	. . .Our Savior. . .
Girl 4	. . .Is he your Savior?
Boy 3	. . .Your Christ?
Girl 2	Have you betrayed Christ?
Boy 2	Have you crucified Christ?
Chorus	What have you done with Christ?

AWAKE OH SLEEPER*

by Sue Lile Inman

Use a spotlight on the soloists to enhance the mood of the selection. Be creative with your arrangement of the readers. Use musical background for the transitions.

Chorus   "Awake, O sleeper, (musical background)
                       and arise from the dead,
              And Christ shall give you light."
              Look carefully then
                   how you walk,
              not as unwise men
                   but as wise,
              making the most of the time,
                   because the days are evil.

Chorus stands and turns completely with backs to audience.

Solo 1   I stood on the brink of the future
              and the world
              fell in fragments at my feet
              in a kaleidoscope of harlot colored pieces of glass
              illumined in the sickly purple light
              of a setting sun.
              Standing I heard the knell of the ages
              whispering down the spiral corridor of the past
              and echoing into the now
              with reverberations of frantic clamor.

Men   "We are the hollow men
              We are the stuffed men
              Leaning together
              Headpiece filled with straw Alas!

Solo 2   "I stood on the Old World streets,
              Amid ruins and rubble.
              And living ruins and breathing rubble
              That spoke like rain on ashes:
              War and again war
              Once a generation.

Reprinted by permission of Sue Lile Inman, and Association Press.

Marching millions
Cheers and tears at the railroad stations
Crutches and coffins for the trip back.
Houses blown into dust.
Cities and nations blown into dust
Shadows on shadowy streets picking over garbage cans.
Love for sale for a cigarette.
Once a generation!
Idiocy, Idiocy!
Everything is a fraud.
God is a fraud.
There is no god but Evil!"

3 girls "Here we go round the prickly pear
go around Prickly pear, prickly pear
bench Here we go round the prickly pear
singing At five o'clock in thc morning."
Solo, Man 1 "Life is very long. . .
Solo Man 2 For Thine is the Kingdom. . .

Solo
Man 3   For thine is
Solo
man 4   Life is
Solo
Man 5   For Thine is the
Women   This is the way the world ends
(Chanting)   This is the way the world ends
          This is the way the world ends
          Not with a bang but with a whimper.
Solo 3   A bomb explodes in the Pacific. . .
          A million namless men die
          On a million nameless streets in Bombay
          Hong Kong, Berlin,
          Detroit. . .
          A Mau Mau tribesman brandishes a bloody
          sword of futile freedom
          over the body of a mutilated mother, and
          a child's wail rends the night. . .
Solo
Woman 1   We, (up and turn around)
Woman 2   You and I, (up and around)

                    woman 3   woman 4
                    move from bridge table, to fraternity
                              woman 5
                        meeting, to TV set,
              woman 6   woman 7
                    to study group, to Sunday sermon
Woman 8   Searching for a purpose. . .
Women   Each a fragment without a pattern
                   a picture without a frame
                   a human without a center.
Chorus   "Has a nation changed its gods
all turn   even though there are no gods?
to front   But my people have changed their glory
                        for that which does not profit.
                   Be appalled, O heavens at this
                        be shocked, be utterly desolate,
                              says the Lord,
                   for my people have committed two evils:
                        they have forsaken me,
                   the fountain of living waters,
                        and hewed out cisterns for themselves
                   broken cisterns, that can hold no water.
Solo 4   Hollywood and Vine, Five Points, Times Square,
                   The Loop. . .
                   Shuffling feet and dead mask eyes from faces
                   on all the corners of America.
Solo 5   Piercing the night with a weird glow
                   a white cross burns
                   before an unpainted shanty in Alabama. . .
Solo 6   A Negro turned
                   from a white church in Chicago
Chorus   Saturday night and aloneness
                   in a single lighted room in a
                   dark dormitory hall. . .
                   at college parties. . .hollow music
                   empty souls. . .
                   blind to ourselves:
                   unaware of the dreadful wail
                   of the world we have never allowed
                        ourselves to see.

                              202

Solo 7   O Lord deliver us,
               we are hollow and incomplete.
               Our world is a half world made pitifully
                  great by science.
               We move among ghost shapes,
               half seeking thy purpose and half content
               with our own comfortable emptiness.
               Father God have mercy upon us.
               Grant us the wholeness
               we see in thy son, Jesus Christ,
               that we might bring to our empty world
               a hope and a promise.
Chorus   Let us rise from worship
               not with His benediction but
               with His call.
               "Now the word of the Lord came to me saying,
               "Before I formed you in the womb I knew you,
               and before you were born I consecrated you;
               I appointed you a prophet to the nations."
               Then I said, 'Ah, Lord God! Behold, I do not
               know how to speak, for I am only a youth.'
               But the Lord said to me,
               'Do not say, "I am only a youth";
               for to all to whom I send you you shall go
               and whatever I command you you shall speak
                  Be not afraid of them,
                   for I am with you to deliver you,
                      says the Lord.'
               Then the Lord put forth his hand and touched
               my mouth; and the Lord said to me
Chorus   'Behold, I have put my words in your mouth,
up   See, I have set you this day over nations
                  and over kingdoms.
               To pluck up and to break down,
               to destroy and to overthrow
               to build and to plant."
                      —Amen

               By Sue Lile Inman, Agnes Scott College

WHAT IS A YEAR*

by Harland Steele

What is a year?
      They say it's a clock
      That doesn't run down
      For 365 ¼ days of 8,766 hours
      Or 525,960 minutes.
   But what of that. . .
      If I'm not thrilled by arithmetic
      Or stirred by statistics?

What is a year?
     They say it's a cycle;
      So many risings of the sun,
      So many fullnesses of the moon,
      So many rotations of the earth.
   But what of that. . .
      If I can only admire heaven's beauty,
      Ignorant of its daily rehearsals?

What is a year?
     They say it's a calendar,
      And certain days mean certain things;
      Some to celebrate, some to fear,
      Some to pay bills, some to sleep-in
   But what of that. . .
      If I'm old and feeble, tied to my bed?
      No moment differs from any other!

What is a year?
     They say it's a unit in aging;
      That men of science can measure,
      That insurance actuaries can figure,
      And doctors ask: "How old are you?"
   But what of that. . .
      If I'm too young, it doesn't bother me;
      If I'm too old, I don't care anymore.

*Reprinted by permission from *The Church Herald*, December 23, 1977.

What is a year?
      Nothing more than arithmetic.
          Cycles
          Calendars
          Aging?
      Has it no meaning
          To life
          To loving
          To longing
      Or just simply to being?

What is a year?
      They say it's events. . .history now.
          Rhodesia, Lebanon War, United Nations,
          SALT meetings, Irishmen fighting.
          Hijacking, Terrorism, Superbowl.
      But what of that. . .
          Is it so new? Plymouth Rock, Civil War,
          Magna Carta, fall of Jerusalem, the Crash.

What is a year?
      They say it's people. . .people now.
          Elvis, Jackie, Amy,
          Muhammed Ali, Farah Fawcett,
          Billy Graham, Archie Bunker.
      But what of that. . .
          The faces are new; the stories old.
          Socrates, Alexander, Pilate, Luther.

What is a year?
      Nothing more than events;
          Things bad
          Things good
          Things neutral?
      Nothing more than people;
          Bad people
          Good people
          No-account people?

What is a year?
>They say it's a fork in the road;
>>A time to set direction,
>>A time to examine purposes,
>>A time to shift gears.
>But what of that. . .
>>Every day is a time of choice!
>>The fool alone waits for the new year.

What is a year?
>They say it's the edge of mystery,
>>An unopened letter, a drawn curtain,
>>A leaping-point into the darkness,
>>The great unknown.
>But what of that. . .
>>Is not each moment a mystery?
>>Is not all of life an unknown?

What is a year?
>Beats me. I wonder if we know.
>Maybe it's all of these. . .
>>Clock
>>Cycle
>>Calendar
>>Aging
>>Events
>>People
>>Fork in the road
>>Mystery.
>Maybe none!

What is a year?
>Just a point in time
>>When you catch your breath,
>>When you can pause to reflect,
>>Whan you take time to wonder.
>Just a point of reckoning;
>>The annual audit,
>>The income tax,
>>The license plate.
>Just an arbitrary point
>>When fools play with fantasy,
>>When failures find scapegoats,
>>When dreamers have hope.

What is a year?
>It's a time like every time;
>>No more important, no less.
>>No more mysterious, no less.
>>No more magic, no less.
>It's a time which is God's time:
>>When the wise man bows his head and says,
>>"Thank you, Lord; you've been good to me."

Narrator	In the beginning God created the heaven and the earth—And God saw the light that it was good and God divided the light from the darkness. And God called the light Day, and the darkness He called Night, and there was evening and there was morning, the first day. And God said, let us make man in our image, after our likeness. So God created man in His own image.
Solo	Was he Catholic, Protestant, or Jew?
Solo	Was he white, yellow, or black? He whom God created in His image?
Chorus	Man was created man./ Different from fish or four-footed animal./ Different in color/ But still man./ Wanting the same things—/
Solo	Food to eat
Solo	A place to sleep.
Solo	Land to work, to live in, to build.
Chorus	A better world for his young/ And he got that better world Because man worked with man/
Solo	to build a home,
Solo	to make the first wheel,
Solo	to bring the first fire,
Solo	and it was man working with man who built the town and the nation.
Solo	The little house and the skyscraper.
Solo	The wagon and the streamliner.
Solo	The arching bridge and the B-29
Chorus	And no one asked/ Was he black or white/ Was he Catholic, or Protestant, or Jew./
Narrator	We built a nation, powerful and glorious, Because man worked with man.
Solo	The English at Plymouth.
Solo	The Dutch at New Amsterdam.
Solo	The Protestants in New England.

Solo	The Catholics in Maryland.
Narrator	And we fought the Revolution
	So man could live with man
	In freedom, in peace
Chorus	And no asked
	At Valley Forge and Saratoga/
	Was he black or white./
	Was he Catholic, or Protestant, or Jew./
Narrator	When the slaves in the South in their pain and suffering cried for freedom, they sang,
Chorus	"When Israel was in Egypt Land,
(sing)	Let my people go
	Oppressed so hard they could not stand.
	Let my people go.
	Go down, Moses, way down in Egypt Land.
	Tell Ole Pharaoh to let my people go."
Solo	The Protestant Negro sang of the yearning
	Of the white Jew for freedom
	Because freedom belongs to all men,
	Not to one color, not to one religion.
Solo	In the pain and suffering in the last war
	Did the wounded Protestant of Iowa
	Fighting in Korea ask
	"Whose blood are you pouring into
	my veins so that I may live?"
Solo	Did the colored gunner cutting his way
	through Italy ask,
	"Who made the gun, who filled this bullet?"
Chorus	No one asks on the firing front/
	Is he black or white.
	Is he Catholic or Protestant or Jew./
Narrator	I went to a movie last week.
Solo	She saw Margaret O'Brien—Irish and Catholic
Narrator	And I wore my new cotton dress.
Voice	The cotton was picked by a colored man in the South
Narrator	I rode by train
Solo	Every race, every color, every religion was in the train with her.

209

Solo	There were some colored children in the train. They were too young to know the misery of a race discriminated against. They were singing an old colored song. They were happy.
Narrator	And then I met a friend. We were hungry and went in for a bite to eat.
Solo	The man who served them was a Swede and Protestant.
Narrator	After the movies I came home, turned on the television, watched my favorite programs.
Chorus	And she saw Danny Thomas, a Jew/Perry Como, a Catholic;/Pat Boone, a Protestant/Marion Anderson, A Negro./
Narrator	And I thought to myself what a wonderful world this was with so many different people helping me to be healthy, and happy, and how much I owed them.
Chorus	And she didn't ask once that day/on the train/ in the movies/in her home./
Light Woman	Is he black or white/is he Catholic or Protestant/ or Jew./
Dark Woman	Will you listen to the one who divides black from white, Protestant from Catholic from Jew?
Solo	What are you missing?
Chorus	Man divided from man/man fighting against man has taken it from you./
Solo	What have you?
Chorus	Man living with man/man working with man gave it to you./
Solo	In all your deeds, in all your thoughts, in all you say, in all you do, remember this
Narrator	"And God created man in His own image, in the image of God created He him,"
Solo	And it doesn't say he was white, it doesn't say he was black, it doesn't say he was Catholic or Protestant or Jew.
Chorus	It just says He created man/That's all of us./

SPECIAL OCCASIONS

Combine your singing choir and your verse choir to present a lovely program for your church on special days. Order "Where Shall I Find the Christ Child," a cantic for speaking choir and mixed singing voices from Abingdon Press, Nashville. An interesting song with guitar accompaniment is "Where's Christmas," available at Lexicon Music, Inc.

TRIUMPHAL MARCH*

Palm Sunday

Chorus
    ^m   ^w   ^m ^w   ^w

Stone/bronze/stone/steel/stone/oakleaves horses' heel over the paving/

     ^w   ^m   Chorus

And the flags and the trumpets. And so many eagles. Chorus

Solo
How many? Count them./And such a press of people./We hardly knew ourselves that day, or knew the City/. This is the way to the temple/, and were so many crowding

Solo
the way. So many waiting, (how many Chorus waiting?) What did it matter, on such a day?

Chorus

Solo
Are they coming?/No, not yet/You can see some

eagles./And hear the trumpets/.

Chorus   Solo
Here they come. Is *he* coming?

*From "Coriolon" in *Collected Poems,* 1909-1962. Copyright 1936, by Harcourt, Brace Jovanovich, Inc.; copyright ©1963, 1964 by T.S. Eliot. Reprinted by permission of the publishers.

Chorus	The natural wakeful life of our ego is a perceiving./
	We can wait with out stools and our sausages/.

solo   solo   solo   Chorus

	What comes first?/Can You see? Tell us. It is
Solo	5,800,000 rifles and carbines,
Solo	102,000 machine guns
Solo	28,000 trench mortars
Solo	53,000 field and heavy guns.
Chorus	I can not tell how many projectiles, mines
	and fuses./
Solo	13,000 aeroplanes,
Solo	24,000 aeroplane engines,
Solo	50,000 ammunition wagons,
Solo	55,000 army wagons,
Solo	11,000 field kitchens,
Solo	1,150 field bakeries.

solo   chorus

W	What a time that took. Will it be he now? No/
	Those are the golf club Captains,/these the scouts,/
	And not the societe gymastique de Poissy/
	And now come the Mayor and the Liverymen./Look
	There he is now/look:/
Solo	There is no interrogation in his eyes
reverently	Or in the hands,/quiet over the horse's neck,/
	And the eyes watchful,/waiting/perceiving,/ indif-
	ferent./
	O hidden under the dove's wind,/hidden in the
	turtle's breast/Under the palm tree at noon/under
	the running water
	At the still point of the turning world./O Hidden,/
Chorus	Now they go up to the temple./Then the sacrifice./
	Now come the virgins bearing urns/urns containing/
Solo	Dust
Solo	Dust

chorus

Solo	Dust of Dust, and now

m   w   m   w   m   w

	Stone, bronze, stone, steel, stone, oakleaves,
Chorus	horses' heels Over the paving./
Quietly	That is all we could see./But how many eagles./
	And how many trumpets./

Solo	(And Easter Day, we didn't get to the country, So we took young Cyril to church, and they rang a bell And he said right out loud, "trumpets.")
	<div align="center">solo</div>Don't throw away that sausage./
	<div align="center">solo solo</div>It'll come in handy./He's artful. Please, will you give us a light?
Chorus	Light/ Light/ Et les soldats faissaient la haie? ILS LA FAISAIENT.

T.S. Eliot

CRUCIFIXION

Solo	And the night/comes again/to the circle/studded sky/
Man	The stars/settle slowly/in loneliness/they lie./
softly	Till the universe explodes/as a falling star/is raised./
	The planets/are paralyzed/the mountains/are amazed./
at be-	But they all/glow brighter/from the brilliance/of the
ginning and	blaze./
build	
	<div align="right">drums</div>
slowly	With the speed/of insanity/then he dies.
Women	In the green fields of Turning a baby is born.
(continue	His cries crease the wind and mingle with the morn.
rhythm)	And the salt upon the orb, the changing of the guard.
	Chosen for a challenge that's hopelessly hard.
	And the only single sign is the sighing of the stars.
	The silence of distance/their song.
Chorus	Images of innocence charge him to go in.
	But the decadence of history is looking for a pawn.
	To a nightmare of knowledge he opens up the gate.
	A blinding revolution is served upon his plate.
	But beneath the greatest love is a hurricane of hate.
	And God help the critic of the dawn.
	(Use a guitar, softly strumming, perhaps something from *Godspell*. Proceed with marked rhythm as verse one is marked.)

Solo Women	So he stands unseen and shouts to the shore. But the louder that he screams the longer he's ignored. For the wine of oblivion is drunk to the dregs. And the merchants of the masses almost have to be begged. Till the giant is aware someone's pulling at his leg. Someone is tapping at the door.
Solo Women	Then his message gathers heed, it spreads across the land. The rewarding of the pain is the following of the man. But the ignorance is everywhere the people have their way. Success is an enemy to the losers of the day. In the shadow of the churches who knows what they pay. And the blood is the language of the band.
Solo Men	The Spanish bulls are beaten—the crowd is soon beguiled. The matador is beautiful, a symphony of style. Excitement is ecstatic, Passion places best. Gracefully he bows to ovations that he gets. But the hands that are upon his are slippery with sweat. Saliva is falling from their smiles.
Chorus drums	So dance/dance/dance/ Teach us to be true./ Dance/dance/dance/ Cause we *love* you./
Woman	And this overflow of light is crushed into a liar. The gentle soul is ripped apart and tossed into the fire. It's the burial of beauty, it's the victory of night. Truth becomes a tragedy living from the light. The heavens are horrified, they stagger from the sight. And the cross is trembling with desire.

Solo W	They say they can't believe it, it's a sacrilegious shame. Now who would want to hurt a hero of the game. But you know I predicted it, I know he had to fall. How did it happen? I hope his suffering was small. Tell me every detail I've got to know it all. And do you have a picture of the pain.

Chorus	Time takes a toll/and the memory fades/
	But his glory/is growing/in the magic/that he made./
	Reality is ruined/there is nothing more to fear./
	This drama is distorted/to what they want to hear/
	Swimming in their sorrow/and the twisting of a tear/.
	As they wait/for the thrill/parade./
	The eyes of the rebel have been branded by the blind
	To the safety of sterility the threat has been refined.
	The child was created to the slaughter house he's led.
	So good to be alive when the eulogies are read.
	The climax of emotion, the worship of the dead.
	As the cycle of sacrifice unwinds.
Chorus	So dance dance dance
drums	Teach us to be true.
	Dance dance dance
	Cause we love you
	And the night comes again to the circle studded sky.
	The stars settle slowly in loneliness they lie.
Solo	'Til the universe explodes as a falling star is raised.
Man	The planets are paralyzed the mountains are
as first	amazed.
verse	But they all glow brighter for the brilliance of the
	blaze. drums cymbals
	With the speed of insanity—then he dies.

EARLY LYNCHING*

Easter

Solo	Two Christs were at Golgotha.
Man	One took the vinegar, another looked on.

One was on the cross, another in the mob.
One had nails in his hands, another the stiff fingers
    holding a hammer driving nails.
There were many more Christs at Golgotha, many more
    their pals, many many more in the mob howling the
    Judean equivalent of "Kill Him! Kill Him!"
The Christ they killed, the Christ they didn't kill,
    those were the two at Golgotha.

Pity, pity, the bones of these broken ankles.
Pity, pity, the slimp of these broken wrists.
The mother's arms are strong to the last.
She holds him and counts the heart beats.

The smell of the slums was on him,
Wrongs of the slums lit his eyes.
Songs of the slums wove in his voice.
But haters of the slums hated his slum heart.

The leaves of a mountain tree,
Leaves with a spinning star shook in them,
Rocks with a song of water, water, over them,

Hawks with an eye for death any time, any time,
The smell and the sway of these were on his
    sleeves, were in his nostrils, his words.

The slum man they killed, the mountain man lives on.

by Carl Sandburg

*From *Modern American Poetry*, Untermeyer, Louis, ed. (c) 1962 by
Harcourt, Brace Jovanovich. Reprinted by permission of the publisher

INDIFFERENCE*

Easter

In this poem which G.A. Studdert-Kennedy wrote, he pictures the contrast between what happened to Jesus in an earlier violent day and what might happen in our 'more kindly' day.

Lm & Lw   When Jesus came to Golgotha they hanged Him on a
        tree/
    They drove great nails through hands and feet,
        and made a Calvary/
    They crowned Him with a crown of thorns/
        red were His wounds and deep/
    For those were crude and cruel days/
        and human flesh was cheap.

Dm & Dw   When Jesus came to Birmingham/they simply passed
        Him by/
    They never hurt a hair of Him, they only let Him die/
    For men had grown more tender, and they would not
        give   Him pain/
    They only just passed down the street/and left him
        in the rain./

Solo   Still Jesus cried, "Forgive them, for they know
        not what
        they do," And still it rained the wintry rain that
        drenched Him through and through;
    The crowds went home and left the Streets without a
        soul to see,
    And Jesus crouched against a wall and cried for Calvary.

by G. A. Studdert Kennedy

*From "The Unutterable Beauty." Reprinted by permission of Hadder and Stroughton.

THE CUP

Easter

M	Stretched out on sloping hill
	By the Garden's gate
	Are ten coarse men/
W	(The most faithful of all) women
M	Cloaks wound under and round,
W	Sleeping,
M	Snoring,
Chorus	Together/
	A stone's throw farther,
	Near the olive trees
	He lies/
	Huddled by a rock,/

      solo M   *solo man*

Beard in hands,/Clothing reeking,/
    Solo M
Pores oozing,/
    solo M
Body writhing,

Chorus	Alone.
Solo M	"My cup runneth over,"
	Boasted Father David
	King of Israel./
Solo M	"Let this cup pass from me,"
	Pleads David's Son,
	King of kings.
Solo 3	"Give me the cup,"
M	Said Socrates of Athens,
	Teacher of truth,/
	As he gulped the hemlock
	And lay down quietly to die.
Solo	"Let this cup pass from me,"
4	Cries Jesus of Nazareth,/
M	The Way and the Truth,/
	As he grovels in the Garden.
Solo	"O God, cannot the cup be spilled, *solo*
W	To seep deep and harmless
	Into Gethsemene's dark earth?"

All	But while the lone one pleads
Women	The cup's already being filled./
M	Judas pockets thirty coins/
	And pours into his Master's cup
	Disillusionment and discontent,/
	A dash of greed;
	He will seal it with a kiss
	And thrust it to his Master's lips./
W	Peter,/sleeping now
	Will pour into the cup
	Before a little servant girl,
	A putrid flow of curse and oath
	Cowardly denial, mouthy shame
	And hold it to his loved one's lips
Chorus	Splendid Pilate, too
	Pouring whimperings
	And finally an order to crucify
	One in whom he found no fault,
	Will call for water/
	To wash the outside clean/
	And hold it to the Galilean's lips/
	The soliders stand erect,/
	With rods and spears and thorny crown,
	Strong, straight limbs from a heavy tree,
	Mallot, whips, and spikes,/
	Vinegar, and blood and water/
	And force it past the stranger's lips,/
Solo	And God himself
W	Has through the years
	Been readying a cup of wrath
	Upon the greed and unbelief of men
	Who have defaced the good,
	Killed the prophets, dirtied love,
	Raped the precious years,
	Spit in their Creator's face

chorus

And cried,/"The earth is man's
and the fullness thereof."/

Solo 1	So God has said,
	I will make ready for the sons of men

Woman 2	A cup of emptiness,
3	A cup of the absence of My Spirit,
4	A cup of eternity without love,
5	Without Light,
6	Without Hope,
7	Without Life.
Chorus	Then the man of Galilee/
	Still wretched in the Garden/
	Looked around for someone else
	To drink the cups of God and man/
Solo 1	Disciples huddled by the gate?
Solo 2	Jews in sleeping holy city?
Chorus	Multitudes on earth inhabiting the cities and mountains of the ages?
Solo 3	You?
Solo 4	I?
Chorus	He wiped away the sweat and blood
	And rose to go to his disciples:/
Solo M	"Rise, let us be going,
	See, my betrayer is at hand."
Chorus	Then strode he
	Out of the Garden
	Into the night/
	Up to skull-hill
	To drain the cup,/
	To empty it
Solo 1	Of death/
Solo 2	Of guilt/
Solo 3	Of wrath/
Solo 4	Of darkness./
Chorus	And, having drunk it to the death/
	To rise again
	And fill the cup for us/
Solo 1	With joy
Solo 2	With hope
Solo 3	With cleansing
Solo 4	With the water of life
Chorus	Which will flow forever
	In the city of God./

G.A. Studdert-Kennedy

A PROGRAM FOR PENTECOST*

Processional

Spirit of Mercy, truth and love
O shed thine influence from above.
And still from age to age convey
The wonders of this sacred day.

Pentecost Acts 2:1-22

W	When the day of the Pentecost had come, they were all together in one place./
M	And suddenly a sound came from heaven
(drum)	like the rush of a mighty wind (drum)
	And it filled the house where they (louder) were sitting./
W	And there appeared to them tongues as of fire/
	Distributed/and resting/on each one of them./
Chorus	And they were all filled with the Holy Spirit and began to speak in other tongues,/
Solo	And the Spirit gave them utterance./
Solo	Now there were dwelling in Jerusalem Jews, Devout men from every nation under heaven.
Chorus	And at this sound the multitude came together. And they were bewildered,/ Because each one heard them speaking in his own language./

Make the saying exciting

And they were amazed, and wondered,/saying
"Are not all these who are speaking Galileans?/
And how is it that we hear, each of us in his own
native language?"/

Look at each other

*From the *Lutheran Hymnal.* © 1941 by Concordia Publishing House. Used by permission.

Chorus	Par/thi/ans
	And Medes and Elamites/
	And residents of Mesopotamia/Judea
	and Cappadocia/
Careful	Pontus and Asia/
rhythm with	
drum	Phrygia and Pamphylia/
	Egypt/
	And the parts of Libya/belonging to Cyrene/
	And visitors from Rome,/both Jews and proselytes,/
	Cretans/and Arabians/
Out of	We hear them telling in our own tongues the mighty
rhythm	works of God/
	And all were amazed and perplexed saying to one another/
Solo	"What does this mean?"
Chorus	But others mocking said
Solo	"They are filled with new wine."
man	
Chorus	But Peter standing with the eleven, lifted up
	his voice and addressed them./
Solo	"Men of Judea and all who dwell in Jerusalem, let
	this be known to you, and give ear to my words.

"For these men are not drunk, as you suppose,
   since it is only the third hour of the day:
   but this is what was spoken by the prophet Joel:
      And in the last days it shall be,
      (God declares) that I will pour out
      my Spirit upon all flesh, and your sons
      and daughters shall prophesy, and your
      young men shall see visions, and your
      old men shall dream dreams.
      Yea, and on my manservants and my maid-
      servants in those days
      I will pour out my Spirit; and they shall
      prophesy. And I will show wonder in the
      heaven above and signs on the earth beneath,
      blood, and fire, and vapor of smoke;
      the sun shall be turned into darkness and
      the moon into blood,
      before the day of the Lord comes,
      the great and manifest day.

And it shall be that whoever calls on the
name of the Lord shall be saved."
(drums—black out)

LOVE AND HATE*

Solo   The sole thing I hate is Hate
For Hate is death: and Love is life
A peace, a splendor from above;
and Hate, a never ending strife
a smoke, a blackness from the abyss
Where unclean serpents coil and hiss!
Love is the Holy Ghost within!
Who preaches otherwise than this
Betrays his Master with a kiss!

by Henry Wadsworth Longfellow

*From *Masterpieces of Religious Verse.* James Dalton Morrison, ed.
©1948. Reprinted by permission of Harper and Row Publishers, Inc.

COME HOLY GHOST, OUR SOULS INSPIRE*

Solo
Come, Holy Ghost, our souls inspire
And lighten with celestial fire
Thou the anointing Spirit art,
Who dost thou seven-fold gifts impart.

Chorus (see below)

Solo
Thy blessed unction from above
Is comfort, life, and fire of love
Enable with perpetual light
The dullness of our blinded sight.

Chorus

Solo
Anoint and cheer our soiled face
With the abundance of thy grace
Keep far our foes, give peace at home
Where thou art guide, no ill can come

Chorus

Chorus
Teach us to know the Father, Son
And Thee, of both, to be but one.
That through the ages all along
This, this may be our endless song;

Chorus

Praise to thy eternal merit
Father, Son, and Holy Spirit.
*(bells, incense, smoke, strobe lights,
then blackout)*

*From *The Lutheran Hymnal* ©1941 by Concordia
Publishing House. Used by permission.

PRAYER

Christmas

Solo   Last night I crept across the snow,
Where only tracking rabbits go,
And then I waited quite alone
Until the Christmas radiance shone!

At midnight twenty angels came,
Each white and shining like a flame.
At midnight twenty angels sang,
The stars swung out like bells and rang.

They lifted me across the hill,
They bore me in their arms until
A greater glory greeted them.
It was the town of Bethlehem.

And gently, then, they set me down,
All worshipping that holy town
And gently, then they bade me raise
My head to worship and to praise.

And gently, then, the Christ smiled down,
Ah, there was glory in that town!
It was as if the world were free
And glistening with purity.

And in that vault of crystal blue,
It was as if the world were new,
And myriad angels, file on file,
Glorified in the Christ-Child's smile.

It was so beautiful to see
Such glory, for a child like me,
So beautiful, it does not seem
It could have been a Christmas dream.

by John Farrar

*From "A Song for Parents" reprinted by permission of Yale University Press.

JOURNEY OF THE MAGI*

Men

A cold coming we had of it/
Just the worst time of the year
For a journey/and such a long journey/
The ways deep and the weather sharp/
The very dead of winter./
And the camels galled, sore-footed, stubborn
Lying down in the melting snow/
There were times we regretted/
The summer palaces on slopes/the terraces/
And the silken girls bringing sherbet/
Then the camel men cursing and grumbling
and running away, and wanting their liquor/
and the night fires going out/and the lack of shelters,/
and the cities hostile and the towns unfriendly
and the villages dirty and charging high prices/
A hard time we had of it/
At the end we preferred to travel all night/
sleeping in snatches,/
with the voices singing in our ears, saying
this was all folly/

Then at dawn we came down to a temperate valley/
wet,/below the snow line, smelling of vegetation/
with a running stream and a water-mill beating the
    darkness
and three trees on the low sky/
And an old white horse galloped away in the meadow/
Then we came to a tavern with vine-leaves over the
    lintel/
six hands at an open door dicing for pieces of silver,
and feet kicking the empty wine-skins./
But there was no information, and so we continued
and arrived at evening, not a moment too soon
finding the place:/it was (you may say) satisfactory/

*From *Collected Poems*, 1909-1962, by T.S. Eliot. Copyrighted 1936
by Harcourt Brace Jovanovich, Inc. copyrighted ©1963, 1964 by T.S.
Eliot. Reprinted by permission of the publisher.

Solo	All this was a long time ago, I remember,
	and I would do it again, but set down
	This set down
	This: were we led all that way for
	Birth or Death? There was a Birth certainly,
	there was evidence and no doubt. I had seen birth and
	death,
	but had thought they were different, this Birth was
	hard and bitter agony for us, like Death, our death.
	We returned to our places, these kingdoms,
	but no longer at ease here in the old dispensation
	with an alien people clutching their gods.
	I should be glad of another death/

by T. S. Eliot

HUMBUG

M	Bah, Humbug some may say—
	So much money spent—too many Santas
W	Making lists/thinking only about receiving/
	Too much tinsel/—too many football games
Chorus	Xmas—hurry—headaches/
	Too much tinsel/too commerical/
Solo 1	Traditional Christmas with Santa Claus—oyster stew—
	programs and trees and candy canes
Solo 2	Stockings and parties and relatives—
	Too many cookies—Too much snow
Solo 3	Red and green—mistletoe and holly—
	Charlie Brown and Frosty the Snowman
Solo 4	Store the decorations for Halloween—
	the candle light—what does it all mean?
LW1	Let this be a Christian Christmas
LM2	Let us have loving and caring
DW3	And praying and sharing
DM4	The star will guide us to the manger.
Chorus	Jesus is born
LW1	He brings hope
LW2	He brings love
DW3	He brings peace
DM4	He brings goodwill (no pauses)

227

A CHRISTMAS PRAYER

Solo

Let us pray that strength and courage abundant be given to
all who work for a world of reason and understanding—that
the good that lies in every man's heart may day by day be
magnified—that men will come to see more clearly not that
which divides them but that which unites them that each
hour may bring us closer to a final victory not of nation over
nation, but of man over his own evils and weaknesses that the
true spirit of this Christmas season—its joy, its beauty, its
hope and above all its abiding faith may live among us that
the blessings of peace be ours—the peace to build and grow,
to live in harmony and sympathy with others and plan for
the future with confidence.

CHRIST CLIMBED DOWN*

Solo   Christ climbed down
from His bare tree
this year
and ran away to where there were
no rootless Christmas trees
hung with candy canes
and breakable stars
Christ climbed down
from His bare tree
this year
and ran away to where there were
  (add voices)

LW   *no gilded Christmas trees*
DW   *and no tinsel Christmas trees*
LM   *and no tinfoil Christmas trees*
DM   *and no gold Christmas trees*

*From Lawrence Ferlinghetti, *A Coney Island of the Mind*.Copyright
©1958 by Lawrence Ferlinghetti. Reprinted by permission of New
Directions Publishing Corporation.

Chorus	*and no black Christmas trees*
	hung with electric candles
	and encircled by tin electric trains
	and clever cornball relatives/
Solo	Christ climbed down
	from His bare tree
	this year and ran away to where
	no intrepid Bible salesman
	covered the territory
	in two-tone cadillacs
LW & LM	and where no Sears Roebuck creches
	complete with plastic babe in manger
	arrived by parcel post/
	the babe by special delivery
DM & DW	and where no televised Wise Men
	praised the Lord Calvert Whiskey
Solo	Christ climbed down
	from His bare tree
	this year and ran away to where
	no fat hand-shaking stranger
	in a red flannel suit
	and a fake white beard/
M	went around passing himself off
	as some sort of North Pole saint
	crossing the desert to Bethlehem
	Pennsylvania
	in a Volkswagon sled/
	drawn by rollicking Adirondack reindeer
	with German names/
	and bearing sacks of Humble Gifts
	from Saks Fifth Avenue/
Chorus	for everybody's imagined Christ Child

Solo

Christ climbed down
from His bare tree
this year
and ran away to where
no Bing Crosby carollers
groaned of a tight Christmas
and where no Radio City angels
ice-skated wingless
through a winter wonderland
into a jingle-bell heaven
daily at 8:30
with Midnight Mass matinees
Christ climbed down
this year
and softly stole away into
some anonymous Mary's womb again
where in the darkest night
of everybody's soul
He waits again
an unimaginable
and impossible
Immaculate Reconception
the very craziest
of Second Comings.

By Lawrence Ferlinghetti

GOD IS HUMAN AFTER ALL

Chorus   They say that Christmas
is no laughing matter.
But I'm not so sure
about that anymore./

Solo   In our house
we sing Silent Night
after the Christmas storm
blows over.

Chorus   God must laugh to himself
at Christmastime.

Solo   Imagine 40 million toys
broken in one day,

Solo   40 million fathers
still assembling
40 million more,

Chorus   and 140 million people
jamming up the stores
that have the spirit
of a Third World War
instead of peace on earth./

Men   Just think of it,

Chorus   40 million glasses of milk
spilled on the good tablecloth
in one day/
40 million mothers
with Christmas headache
numbers 6 or 7/

Men   and just as many fathers
with rather heavy hangovers
from Christmas cheer/of heaven
left on earth./

Solo	I hope you have a sense of humor, God, as you watch our Christmas antics. But when I think of the birth of Christ and everything that happened I know that God was smiling to himself in a very human way.
Chorus	Imagine 40 millions angels frightening tired lazy shepherds camping out one night/
Men	or 40 dirty shepherds

solo   solo solo   solo   solo   chorus

smelly, hairy, bleary, scared, shivering, sleepy shepherds

poking their heads
through the door of a shed/
to look for a baby/
in the middle of the night./

Solo	Imagine a baby bounced on a bony donkey for miles and miles with the help of a carpenter's hands, pierced and rough and raw.
Solo	Imagine a new born baby with a red blotchy face, closed puffy eyes, screaming open mouth, healthy little bowels
Chorus	and call it/ the son of God.
Chorus	Think of it and smile! God became a human being like that./ God became one of us and survived./ God became like me./

Chorus	Think of it and cry./ The son of God is born
Solo	and 40 children die because of Herod's fear.
Chorus	You and I are born while 40 million people die of hunger every year./
Chorus	Think of it and dance./ For God's sense of humor is nothing else but love/
M W	a love that hurts and a love that laughs./
Solo	Now God knows the joy of being human after all.
Solo	God was grafted into Adam's family tree.
Chorus *all*	Think of it,/
soft	and smile./

christmas: st. louis

Chorus	before you get the house in order/the tree-lights untangled/and all your packages wrapped and labeled/i thought i should write and tell you that Jesus was already seen this year by a friend in the middle of a crowd at a stop light downtown/
Chorus	he was in a greyhound bus headed for chicago/

Solo   my friend waved but Jesus did not seem to
              notice him/he was staring at the sky and he
              looked very tired and sad/my friend said we
              should let everybody know before they waste a
              lot of time shopping and cleaning and getting
              ready/that Jesus has come and gone to another
              city./

                              by luke

                         Long Long Ago

Winds thro' the olive trees
    Softly did blow,
Round little Bethlehem
    Long, long ago.

Sheep on the hillside lay
    Whiter than snow;
Shepherds were watching them,
    Long, long ago.

Then from the happy sky,
    Angels bent low,
Singing their songs of joy,
    Long, long ago.

For in a manger bed,
    Cradles we know,
Christ came to Bethlehem,
    Long, long ago.

                         Unknown

Fall on Your Knees, by Dr. Ailene Cole.

FALL ON YOUR KNEES*

(The verse choir and mixed chorus appear on stage as shown
in the picture following the script. All pageant aspects of the
script took place back of the scrim-covered window center
back. Centered back of the window are a cross and a star
which light up red and blue respectively. Two inexpensive
General Electric reflector spots are installed in the ceiling
above the pageant area. One is white light; the other, light
blue. Several 7 watt lamps are installed on the backing
framework of the two stained glass windows. The sign "Peace
on Earth" also lights up. Light cues appearing through the
script are adapted to the facilities of our stage which include

*Reprinted by permission of Dr. Ailene Cole, Director of Theatre,
Augustana College.

red, white, and blue borders and beam lights. The white borders and the beams are dimmed. As the curtains open only the blue and red border lights are on.)

Mixed Chorus: O holy night: the stars are brightly shining,
It is the night of the dear Savior's birth;
Long lay the world in sin and error pining. . .
(Continue in a hum under the verse choir and gradually fade out.)

Verse Choir:　(Beams come on very gradually)

O holy night, O night of hope, O hope born long ages past and kept alive and bright in hearts like yours and mine—in hearts that *dared* to hope despite despair and war and sin, that dared to believe in a purpose for the universe.

Like you and me, those people who heard the words of prophecy had their heartaches and their problems; like us too they were no doubt beset by ultra-realists and scoffers. Yet somehow, they must have felt the touch of a Creator's hand in the gentle caress of the wind, heard His voice in the carol of a bird, and sensed His handiwork in the miracle of the seasons. Because the spark of the Divine in them cried out for something beyond human love to believe and worship, they opened their hearts to the prophecies of a Savior for the world. The Divine spark in their hearts warmed to the glow of eternal love in the Divine promise, and like two pieces of flint lighted a fire of hope that has never died.

O holy night, O holy hope, O prophecy of love.

(Prophet appears in window with scroll and in costume. White spot on. Beams down.) (Mixed Chorus hums while the prophet reads.)

Prophet:　I see him, but not now;
I behold him, but not nigh;
There shall come forth a star out of Jacob (star on)
And a secptre shall rise out of Israel. (Numbers 24:1

236

Behold a virgin shall conceive and bear a son and shall call His name Immanuel. . .For unto us a Child is born; unto us a Son is given; and the government shall be upon His shoulder; and His name shall be called Wonderful, Councillor, the Mighty God, the Everlasting Father, the Prince of Peace. Of the increase of His government and of peace, there shall be no end. . .The zeal of Jehovah of hosts will perform this. (cross on for next portion) He was despised and rejected of men; a man of sorrows and acquainted with grief. . .But He was wounded for our transgressions. He was bruised for our iniquities; the chastisement of our peace was upon Him: and with His stripes we are healed.

(Star, cross, and spot off; beams up gradually)

Verse Choir

Though they could understand but darkly, though they would have had trouble explaining just exactly what they believed, yet—they believed. The words of prophecy were like a soft hand on their aching brows, they brought a quietness and peace to their troubled hearts, they put order into their lives—and they believed—and waited.

As the stars, steadfast and comforting then as now, watched the years in their passing, there came a time when they shone down on Cyranius as governor of Syria and on Caesar Augustus then holding sway at Rome. This was the time. This was it. Yet there was nothing unusual or even promising in the events that preceded that night—that holy night. It seems that even then as now, taxes are levied. So it happened that Caesar Augustus decreed that all should be taxed. Now among those who struggled their weary way to register and to pay the fee was the subject of all the ancient prophesies—the one about to end the long night of waiting. For as Mary and Joseph went patiently on their way to Bethlehem, a star was rising in the East—and in our hearts.

Shall we look back across two thousand years and watch it rise?

(Beams off leaving only red and blue borders on.)

Mixed Chorus: O holy night! The stars are brightly shining:
It is the night of the dear Savior's birth.
(Hum under verse choir. As the gospel is
read by the verse choir, the chorus hums
appropriate carols.)

(Star on.)

Verse Choir:

And it came to pass while they were there, the days were
fulfilled that she should be delivered. And she brought forth
her first-born son, and wrapped Him in swaddling clothes,
and laid Him in a manger—because there was no room at the
inn.

(Pageant in window: three shepherds and in a moment the
angel. Blue spot on the group.)

And there were in the same country shepherds abiding in
the field, keeping watch over their flock by night. And lo, the
angel of the Lord came upon them, and the glory of the Lord
shone round about them, and they were sore afraid. And the
angel said unto them, "Fear not, for behold, I bring you good
tidings of great joy which shall be to all people. For unto you
is born in the city of David a Savior which is Christ the Lord.
And this shall be a sign unto you: You shall find the Babe
wrapped in swaddling clothes, lying in a manger." (Angel
speaks these words.)
And suddenly there was with the angel a multitude for the
heavenly host praising God and saying, "Glory to God in the
highest, and on earth peace, good will toward men." (In the
preceding section, angels as shown in the picture appeared.
"Peace on Earth" sign on.)
And it came to pass as the angels were gone away from
them into Heaven, the shepherds said one to another, "Let us
go even unto Bethlehem and see this thing which the Lord
hath made known unto us."

And they came with haste and found Mary and Joseph and the Babe lying in a manger. . .

(Shepherds enter, kneel, and exit. Wise men enter.)

And behold, Wise Men from the East came saying, "Where is he that is born King of the Jews, for we saw His star in the East and come to worship Him. . .And lo, the star went before them till it came and stood where the young Child was. And they came and saw the young Child with Mary, His mother; and they fell down and worshipped Him; and opening their treasures, they offered unto Him gifts, gold and frankincense and myrrh.

(Wise Men exit. Joseph then exits leaving Mary.)

And Mary kept all these things and pondered them in her heart.)

(Short humming interlude to end the carols.)

Verse Choir: O holy night, O night of love, O night of joy. . .and tears.

(The following poem is divided between the verse choir and Mary. The whole is reinforced with humming.)

Verse Choir: Behold, this child is set for a sign.

Mary: "Nay, but He is so helpless and so sweet,
                Why it is nothing more than if I pressed
                An armful of white roses to my breast,
                Why should a dream I dreamed destroy my rest?"

Verse Choir: Yet even as she spake, she felt the stir
                Of wings that in the manger passed her by.

Mary: "He is so small, so weak against my heart,
                A little wounded dove were as strong as He.
                He hath no other need than need of me,
                Not any life from my own life apart.
                Why should I dread an olden prophecy?"

Verse Choir: Yet even as she spoke, she felt like flame,
                A voice that in the manger said her name.

Mary: "As lesser mothers are, am I not blest,
                He is no other's but mine own, mine own;
                No king, no prophet, but my child alone,
                Asking no other kingdom than my breast.
                Let me be glad these foolish fears are done."

Verse Choir: Yet even as she spake, He stirred in her embrace
                Feeling her tears, her tears—upon His face.
                (The Tears of Mary—Theodosia Garrison)

(Blue light off. Only the red and blue borders on, as well as the church window, the sign, and a star.)

Verse Choir: O holy night, O night of joy—and tears. But what joy is not made sweeter by tears? O nights of thirty-three years that follow—holy nights and days when God's own Son walked upon the earth—our earth—making His mark on those few who were to keep that Bethlehem star shining across the centuries, shining in our hearts today. At length we see Him tracing His way to Jerusalem, resolutely facing the crucifixion at the hands of those He came to serve and love, seeking ease and solace in the garden before being taken for a paltry sum of money.

(Tableau of Christ kneeling in the garden, His hands clasped on a stone, as in the picture so often seen in churches. White spot shines on Him. Voice of an unseen boy reads the following poem and the mixed choir hums.)

BALLAD OF TREES AND THE MASTER*

Boy Solo:

Into the woods my Master went,
Clean forespent, forespent,
Into the woods my Master came
Forespent with love and shame;
But the olives they were not blind to Him;
The little grey leaves were kind to Him;
The thorn tree had a mind to Him
When into the woods He came.

Out of the woods my Master went,
And He was well content.
Out of the woods my Master came
Content with death and shame.
When Death and Shame would woo Him last.
From under the trees they drew His last.
'Twas on a tree they slew Him last (cross on)
When out of the woods He came.

Sidney Lanier

*From a *Little Treasury of American Poetry*, Oscar Williams, ed.
Copyright © 1952. Reprinted by permission of Charles Scribner's Sons.

(All lights off except the star, the cross, and the church windows. Thunder and lightning followed by stillness and the quiet voice of an unseen boy soloist who uses microphone as do all the other soloists. Mixed chorus hums.)

Solo:

Father, forgive them for they know not what they do.

Behold the hour cometh—yes, is come, that ye shall leave me alone; and yet I am not alone because the Father is with me. These things I have spoken unto you that in Me ye may have peace. In the world ye have tribulations; but be of good cheer; I have overcome the world.

Why seek ye the living among the dead. He is not here: he is risen.

In my Father's house are many mansions. I go to prepare a place for you.

Fear not, for lo I am with you always, even unto the end of the world.

I am the resurrection and the life; he that believeth on me, though he were dead, yet shall he live; and whosoever liveth and believeth in me shall never die.

Peace I leave with you; my peace I give unto you.

Verse Choir: O holy night, O blessed morn.
              O slender Christ upon the cross
              Those wistful eyes are sad and shaped for tears.
              What have we done of all that you commanded?
              Little enough these last two thousand years.

(from *The Crucifix* by Laurence Hope)

So little that a poet today writes: (Church window lights off.)

TO JESUS ON HIS BIRTHDAY*

Boy's Voice: (Unseen)

For this your mother sweated in the cold. (Star off)
For this you bled upon the bitter tree;
A yard of tinsel ribbon bought and sold;
A paper wreath; a day at home for me.
The merry bells ring out, the people kneel;
Up goes the man of God before the crowd;
With voice of honey and with eyes of steel
He drones your humble gospel to the proud.
Nobody listens. Less than the wind that blows   (Sing
                                                  off on
                                                  listens.)

Are all your words to us you died to save.
O Prince of Peace! O Sharon's dewy Rose!
Hou mute you lie within your vaulted grave. (Cross off)
The stone the angel rolled away with tears
Is back upon your mouth these thousand years.

Verse Choir:

The stone the angel rolled away with tears
Is back upon your mouth these thousand years.

by Millay

*From *Collected Poems.* Harper and Row. Copyright
1928,1955 by Edna St. Vincent Millay.

Repeating these words of condemnation, my spirit cries in protest: "No, it cannot be." Yet, there is the challenge to the very foundation of my living—of my universe.

In my need to fling back my answer to the poet's challenge clearly and simply, I go out and walk under the stars. Always from them I gain ease and reassurance when unnamed longings stir my soul. And tonight as always, their order and punctuality speak of a Master Creator whose simplest thought is farther from our understanding than any one of these stars. As I gaze at them robed in sparkling blue, delicate rose, or lush off-white, I tune in on the heavenly plan of harmony and beauty. . .So as I walk along in the snowy whiteness of a winter night, my soul finds peace—and light again. (Sign on) And I raise my eyes and heart in mute thankfulness for sermons stronger than words, for comfort thousands of light-years old, yet ever new. O handiwork of God—O holy message retold nightly in brilliant starlines—for all who lift their eyes and hearts to see. (Star on.)

Coming back to the now. I see that the need for answering the challenge in words is less insistent—because once more in my heart I know—I know the voice of Jesus speaks to us every day. And I ask: Need we explain our faith? Isn't it truer worship just to feel the peace and hope of the simple Christmas story?

Feeling this peace, I realize in a blinding flash of understanding that beneath our brusque exteriors is an inner sensitivity and need we keep hidden and that our daily routines are just outlines into which we fit our soul's living. It is that universe of inner reality which is the kingdom of the Christ Child—it is the kingdom of the heart He came to serve—is serving—will serve. And it is there that he is heard.

O Christ of the manger and the empty tomb. (Cross on) we open our hearts to you—unashamed —and listen in the perfect trust of a child. Yes, a little child. Think of an infant completely dependent on its parents, trusting them, and filling in their hearts a corner as big as a universe. Oh no, the stone has not rolled back upon the lips of the risen Jesus. He speaks to every dad and mother through their own child; and

His command to love one another is obeyed in a love too tender for the day to trace, as there is the miracle of a new life they know there is a purpose for the universe.

Time passes and I see sturdy little legs of brother and sister trudging hand in hand to Sunday School, learning to sing "Jesus Love Me" in the strange unblended harmony of childish voices. I hear a childish voice in perfect trust talking with the infant Jesus, in trusting childish tones.

Solo: (Primary girl in sleepers kneeling. Mixed chorus hums.)

Beams off: blue spot on).

A CHILD'S PRAYER

Little Jesus, wast Thou shy
Once, and just as small as I?
And what did it feel like to be
Out of Heaven and just like me?
Didst Thou sometimes think of There
And ask where all the angels were?
I should think that I would cry
For my house all made of sky:
I would look about the air
And wonder where my angels were;
And at waking 'twould distress me—
Not an angel there to dress me.

Didst Thou kneel at night to pray
And didst Thou join Thy hands, this way?. . .
I used to think, before I knew,
The prayer not said unless we do.

And did Thy mother at the night
Kiss Thee and fold the clothes in right?
And didst Thou feel quite good in bed,
Kissed, and sweet, and Thy prayers said?
Thou canst not have forgotten all
That it feels like to be small.
So a little Child, comes down
And hear a child's tongue like Thy own;
Take me by the hand and walk
And listen to my baby talk.
To Thy Father show my prayer
(He will look, Thou art so fair)
And He will smile that children's tongue
Has't not changed since Thou wast young?

by F. Thompson

(Spot off.)

Voice of Jesus: Suffer the little children to come unto Me and forbid them not, for to such belongeth the kingdom of Heaven.

(Beams up a bit.)

Verse Choir:

Inspired by this simple faith, I turn next to the adult world where complex modern living, frightening and awe-inspiring scientific discoveries, youthful dreams fading in the distance, and death looming closer in the future all cry out the world's *need* for God's peace and beauty. And springing from that carefully hidden kingdom of the heart come by-products of the mouth of Christ speaking. Kindnesses done for the sheer joy of the doing, a united community searching for one child that is lost like the shepherd leaving the ninety-nine for the one, smiles and works of friendship and of comfort—these tell of a people letting the voice of the Chirst Child in them speak through their actions.

Seeing this in the heart kingdom of my fellowmen, I give thanks to the poet who aroused me to negative defense of the star which lights our lives. And isn't that action the answer? Isn't it living deeply in the Christ Child's kingdom in our hearts that fills our lives, not just mouthing the words and going through the motions but feeling and living them—every day?

As the Voice of the Christ caresses my needy soul in response, I relax in the hush of His peace—and into my spirit steal the words of the Arabian poet through whom the risen Lord has spoken to countless thousands. Listen!

Boy Solo: (In costume. Beams off: white spot on.)

> Is not religion all deed and all reflections?
> Who can separate his faith from his actions, or his belief
>   from his occupation?
> Who can spread his hours before him, saying, "This is for
>   God and this for myself; this for my soul and this
>   other for my body?
> Your daily life is your temple and your religion.
> When you enter into it, take with you your all.
> Take your plow and the forge and the mallet and the lute
> And take with you also men;
> For in aspiration you cannot fly higher than their hopes nor
>   humble yourself lower than their despair,
> And if you would know God, be not therefore a solver
>   of riddles.
> Rather look about you and you shall see Him playing with
> your children.
> And look into space; you shall see Him walking in the cloud,
>   outstretching His arms in the lightning and ascending in
>   the rain.
> You shall see Him smiling in flowers, then rising and waving
>   His hands in trees.

(from *The Prophet* by Kahlil Gibran)*

(spot off; keep beams off.)

Verse Choir:

O holy night—O blessed Christ, reach out your hands from the cradle and the grave and in the stillness and the hush of this night, give us peace and understanding. Let us see the light of our lives—aglow and warm with holy love.

(Blue spot on. Manger tableau with angels)

Verse Choir:

Glory to God in the highest—and on earth peace, good will toward men.

(While the Mixed Chorus sings "O Holy Night" the chorus and the verse choir form a huge cross formation facing the tableau. On "Fall on your knees," all kneel.

Boy's Voices:

> Deep peace of the running wave to you,
> Deep peace of the flowing air to you,
> Deep peace of the quiet earth to you,
> Deep peace of the shining stars to you,
> Deep peace of the watching shepherds to you,
> Deep peace of the Son of Peace to you.
> Amen

(An old Gaelic rune.)

ADDITIONAL RECOMMENDATIONS

BIBLIOGRAPHY

AND

INDEX OF TITLES

ADDITIONAL RECOMMENDATIONS

"Praise the Lord"—an excellent processional with music. Order from Tyndale House Publisher, Wheaton, Illinois, 60187.

"Fugue of Nations"—A speaking chorus. Order from Lexicon Music, Inc.

"Where Shall I Find the Christ Child?" Max Exner (a cantic for speaking choir and singing voices) Abingdon Press.

"Where's Christmas?" Words and music by Tedd Smith, Lexicon Music, Inc.

"Chortos I" (anthem for Speech Choir.) Texts from the Old and New Testaments. Music by Richmond Browne, Harold Flammer, Inc. Delaware Water Gap, Pa. 18327.

"Cry Out and Shout" (for special choir and snare drum) by Ben Ludlow. Harold Flammer, Inc.

"Gotta be Spring," (for 2-part speech choir) by Ben Ludlow. Shawnee Press, Inc.

"List Whist," by E.E. Cummings (for speech choir of mixed voices) Shawnee Press, Inc.

BIBLIOGRAPHY

Aggertt, Otis J. and Elbert R. Brown.*Communicative Reading.* New York: Macmillan Co., 1963.

Albright, Hardie. *Acting: The Creative Process.* Belmont, California: Dickerson Publishing Co., 1967.

Bacon, Wallace A. *The Art of Interpretation.* New York: Holt, Rinehart and Winston, Inc., 1966.

Boleslavsky, Richard.*Acting, The First Six Lessons.* Theatre Arts, 1949.

Coger, Leslie Irene and Melvin R. White. *Readers Theatre Handbook.* Glenview, Illinois: Scott Foresman and Co., 1967

Cole, Ailene.*The Aims and Techniques of Choral Reading.* Unpublished Master of Arts Thesis, University of Minnesota, 1940.

Crocker, Lionel and Louis Mr. Eich, *Oral Reading.* New York; Prentice-Hall, Inc., 1955.

Duerr, Edwin. *The Length and Depth of Acting.* New York: Holt, Rinehart and Winston, Inc., 1962.

England, Gene *Relaxation* (A casette tape with exercises in Relaxation) Behavioral Sciences Institute, 72 Fern Canyon Road Carmel, Calif. 93921.

Franklin, Miriam A. *Rehearsal.* Englewood Cliff, New Jersey: Prentice Hall, Inc.,1963.

Garner, Dwight L. and Ralph L. Beckett. *Speech Dynamics.* Dubuque, Iowa: Wm. C. Brown Co., 1967.

Grim, Harriet Elizabeth. *Practical Voice Training.* New York: Appleton-Century Crafts, Inc., 1948.

Grims, William H. and Alethea Smith Mattingly. *Interpretation, Writer, Reader, Audience.* San Francisco: Wadsworth Publishing Co., Inc.,1961.

Kahan, Stanley. *Introduction to Acting.* New York: Harcourt, Brace and World, Inc.,1962.

Langer, Susanne K. *Philosophical Sketches.* New York: A Mentor Book published by New American Library, 1964.

————. *Philosophy in a New Key.* New York: A Mentor Book published by New American Library of World Literature, Inc.,1964.

———— *Reflection on Art.* Oxford University Press N.Y., 1961.

Lee, Charlotte J. *Oral Interpretation.* 3d ed. Boston: Houghton Mifflin Co., 1965.

Lowrey, Sara and Gertrude E. Johnson. *Interpretative Reading.* New York: Appleton-Century Crafts, Inc., 1942.

McGaw, Charles. *Acting is Believing.* New York: Holt, Rinehart and Winston, 1960.

Moore, Sonia. *The Stanislavsky Method.* New York: The Viking Press, 1960.

"Now Relax,"*The Des Moines Register,* March 9, 1967.

Owen, Mary Gwen. "If You Are Planning a Choral Reading," *Minnesota Journal of Education.* 21:402 (May, 1941).

———— "An Approach to the Teaching of Choral Speech," *Minnesota Journal of Education.* 19:383, 85 (May, 1939).

Parrish, Wayland Maxfield. *Reading Aloud.* New York: The Ronald Press Co., 1953.

Povenmire, E.K. "Sabbatical Study Tour Reports." Unpublished report, 1964-1965.

INDEX OF TITLES

ABOUT THE AUTHOR

Dr. Theora C. England was born in Kansas and raised in Missouri and Iowa, where her father was a preacher and professor of the Bible and languages. She received her B.A. from Simpson College and her M.A. and Ph.D. from the University of Minnesota. From Northwestern College she received an honorary Doctor of Dramatic Arts degree.

Dr. England married Mr. Harry England (deceased 1968), with whom she raised two sons. Presently the author is a retired college professor and lives in Iowa. She has organized and directed choral reading groups in South Carolina and Tennessee.

Her son Frederick is a chemical engineer with Texaco at Houston, Texas, and her son Gene is president of the Behavioral Sciences Institute of Carmel, Calif.